Third Annual
Northwoods Anthology

Dan,
Let's get together soon and
talk about writing. Call me,
My number is 651-777-1465.
Fred

Compiled by

Robert W. Olmsted

My story starts on p. 70, and
it's pretty good. But be sure
to read the first story in
the book. It's great,

ISBN 0-89002-383-2 // $16.95

Fiction & Poetry

All works were proofed by their own authors.

Northwoods Press
The Poet's Press
Thomaston, Maine

Contents

Mademoiselle Fleur

Peter Owens
Marstons Mills, MA

So ees very dark, and I come to steal my boat. Was belong to Papa, rest his soul, but dat RCMP says, "Pierre Louis (that's me), thees boat ain't belong to you. It belong to da government."

I says, "Git da hell off my boat." and they says it ain't belong to you and they put dat sign up, *Confisqué.*

"My papa, hees soul come down from heaven and curse you guy," I yells, so dat RCMP hurry quick wid da sign and tell to me, "You on dis boat tomorrow, go to jail, Pierre Louis."

"Ahhhh," I say and point to papa in da sky, and da RCMP he jump off da boat and cross hees self and kiss da thumb, den wag da finger at me.

Jeez.

So I take da boat and I sail out Saint John after midnight. Everyting I leave. Don't tell no one. I go to U.S.

Big wind dat night. Go like hell. After dat night, nice wind dat. Go good. Smoke Cuban cigar. Very good dis.

I go Fairhaven. Sound good, dat name, hey? Fairhaven. Across da bay ees New Bedford. Good place that. Wild place. Easy get lost. Many outlaw there. Long way to Canada.

Mademoiselle Fleur, she fine boat. Go fast. Papa know dis boat. Work his life keep her good. Like new. Damned good boat. So he don't pay no government. Dey give him to the boat. Give ever-ting after big crash, 1929. Now dey want to steal Papa boat. No own *Mademoiselle Fleur*, they say me. RCMP too many lazy. *Confisqué*, ha! Don't know Pierre Louis.

Nice down here to New Bedford. Warm. Many boat. All up and down da wharf. Big red-top guy call him Sully. "Heah," he yell. I tie up at da wharf and hold money for Sully. He laugh. "We don't take that Canuck shit," he laugh. No many teeth, dis guy. Lots of fight, dis guy. Very strong.

"Pay latuh," Sully say. Big smile, dis guy.

"Who dat Latuh?"

He laugh. Wave me bye-bye and go up da wharf and grab dis pretty girl, she try to run away and she slap him, and Sully he slap dat girl in de mouth. Hard. Ouch.

She young girl, fourteen, fifteen, maybe and she ain't more dan hundred pounds all wet, so I yell Sully.

"Hey, dat girl. She my crew, dat girl."

He look me and give me the F sign, and da girl, nose bleed and she try crawl away, and Sully try kick to her bum, and he slip, fall on hees bum, grab ankle to da girl, and jump up quick, dis guy. He pick up dis girl wid da fist. Big guy, dis Sully, haul girl down da wharf to *Mademoiselle Fleur* and heave her like da rag doll on my deck.

"She's a bloody thief, and you tell the little snitch Sully will shoot her dead next time. You got that, French fry?" Sully turn and take big stride off da wharf.

Jeez.

Dis how I meet Rosa. Very good luck, this. We good pair, me and Rosa.

She good worker. Come from da mills in Fall Rivers. Fix da sail. Splice da line.

I pay Rosa good money, and we do good.

American lobster da same. Go in pot. Get lost. No get out. Not so smart, hey.

José pay good price. I pay Sully. He leave Rosa alone. Wave to her. Say hi. Sully take care of da wharf HIS wharf. Rosa okay now. She my crew. Sully tell the boys. Rosa, she belong to *Mademoiselle Fleur.*

I like Rosa, but I am very shy. I tell to her, "Hey, Rosa, you gotta pretty brown eyes just like da cow."

Rosa swat me good.

Jeez.

She learn to sail. "Jesus, Louis (Lew-eeeey is how she say me). This G-D tub won't turn," she say.

"Make some speed," I say.

"I can't," she yell above the flutter of da sail.

"Not into da wind, Rosa, my Rosa. Fall off da wind."

"I ain't falling off nowhere," she say. "Louis!" she scream.

It don't take long and Rosa sail good. Better dan most man. Dis work good. Rosa she sail and me I haul da pots. All day. Sometime very late.

I watch Rosa sail. Pretty girl. Smart. I like dis girl.

Sometime I go below and drink whiskey. Try to get da courage, hey? Try to say, hey Rosa, hey my Rosa, you pretty girl, pretty woman. I say dis many time in my head. Look in da mirror to shave. Pretend ees Rosa and not ugly Pierre Louis. Very pretty woman. I say dis in my head. No dare say to Rosa.

One day dis nasty guy from Fall Rivers come. He say he want Rosa. Rosa belong to him, he say. Rosa very scared, very angry, tell dis guy to F-off. He grab Rosa arm, and I grab da man neck, and he pull da knife and stick under my chin.

Sully come running. "Git yer ass off my dock!" Sully yell to the Fall Rivers guys.

Da man push dat knife and cut hole under my chin. Not too much deep. *Mais* lots da blood. Turn to go. He spit on *Mademoiselle Fleur*. "I'm coming back," he says. "I'll bring the priest."

I bleeding all over da place. Rosa cry. Sully try explain me. Rosa try explain me. Most she sniffle and howl. Jeez.

Back den, she live in da convent with da nuns. Da priest send Rosa to work da mills. Good money. Send all da girls.

"They sign da contract," Sully say. "Ain't nothing you can do." Sully swears terrible tings about da priests. All da priests. All da nuns. I look up da sky. No lightening. Jeez. Lucky.

Da next Friday night we sail in da wharf. Beat da big storm. Full da lobsters. José many happy man. Lots of monies. "You guys are the best," shout José to me and Rosa. He bring da boys to offload. Give me five bottle da whiskey, lots of monies. Big day down to Sully's wharf. Lots of boat. Many big load. Swordfish, flounder, cod, haddock. Many whiskeys. Many monies. José get very drunk. I get drunk. Rosa drunk. Sully drunk. All da man, all da crews. Big party down der before da big storm.

Then dat man come with da priests and he bring hees friend, many friend.

Dey march down da wharf, and all the noise and yelling and cussing stop.

Rosa clutch my arm. I feel her tremble. She don't like dis. She don't like dem guys.

Dat priest steps my plank on *Mademoiselle Fleur*. He say, "Come home now, Rosa, dear." Many sugars in dat voice.

Rosa, she clutch me hard and hide her head behind my shoulder.

"Rosa work for me, Fader," I say da priest.

"Not legally, I'm afraid, my son." More sugars in dat voice. "She is obligated to these men until she is 21-years-old or married. She has no choice is this matter. I'm so sorry, my dear."

Rosa, she begin to sob. All da men watch. Dey quiet. Far away rumble in da black sky.

"You marry me, hey," I say to da sugar priest.

"You want me to marry you?" da priest laugh.

"Ah oui yes," I say. What is this priest to laugh at me?

Rosa tug on my arm and peek her head around.

"Pierre Louis means he wants you to marry us," she say da priest.

"Ah yes, yes, oui," I say. "Rosa and Pierre Louis, meester and missus Lew-eeeyy."

I turn Rosa. I very excite now. Very nervous. "Yes, thees okay, Rosa?"

"Yes," she say. Then she wrap arms around me, and all de men, they cheer and whistle, and the sugar priest, he smile, and them boys he come with, they scowl and shuffle.

"You can't do this," yell da bad one. He grab da priest by da arm and yank him around.

Lots of hoots and hisses from all da men, from all da boats from all da docks.

Fader not happy now. No sugar now. He look at dat bad man. "I will do what is right under the laws of God and the Church," he say to da bad guy.

Sully push through all the bad boy. "How about it, Father. Right now's a good time for a wedding."

"Well, I suppose, given the circumstances. You are Catholic?" he ask me.

"Yes oui. Yes, I be many big Catholic."

"To marry right now? Is this okay with you, Rosa?" da sugar priests ask.

"Hmmm. Yes, Father," she say. Big smile she.

"And you, sir?" he ask me.

"Ah, *oui*. Perfect," I say him.

Da bad boys mutter and grumble but don't dare curse da priest. Dey scowl at da bigging crowd of New Bedford peoples coming to meet da boats and finding a wedding surprise.

He take Rosa below for confession. Soon she come out. Big smile she. "Your turn," she tell me.

"Hey, Sully. Don't let them bad men near my Rosa," I tell to him.

"We won't let 'em budge," Sully say, so I go below and take off da hat and bow.

"Bless me, Fader."

"Kneel, my son."

"Ah oui, sorry." I kneel down and cross myself. "Bless me, Fader. I have sin."

But I can't think of no sin.

"When did you last confess?"

"Ah. A year? About year maybe, maybe more, *oui*."

"Since then have you used the Lord God's name in vain?"

"No-no. Not me, Fader. I use some bad word, hey. I use da F-word, and I use da S-word. Some time da B-word. Not so bad, Fader. Not too much, hey. Not a big sin, hey?"

"But you do swear sometimes?"

"Sometime, maybe. Not too much."

"I have to ask you if you've sinned with Rosa."

"No-no. No-no. Not me sin Rosa, nossir, Fader, not a lettle bit even."

"Well, then, have you sinned in your mind with Rosa?"

"Not too much, Fader."

"You haven't touched her lewdly in your mind?"

"Oh, no-no, Fader. I not do that to Rosa. I am not dat man, hey."

"But you said 'not too much.' What did you mean by that?"

"I keess her. A leetle bit. Not too much. Sometime, I keess her in my mind, Fader. I look in the mirror and I tell to her she ees very beautiful, very sexy. But thees is to me, not to her. Not that same, hey."

"I see. Not too much then. I see. All right, then, can I ask you if you have stolen since your last confession?"

"Oh, no, no, no. No, Fader. I am not a thief."

"You've not stolen from or cheated anyone?"

"Ah wait, Fader. Da boat. I stole da boat."

"What boat?"

"Theese boat. Not really steal. *Mais,* yes, Fader, I steal da boat. You see, theese my papa's boat. Forty year. Da government give papa dat boat. 1929. Big crash. Give papa da boat. Last year papa die. Government come. Say da boat ain't for me. Don't belong to me. Hey, Fader, me and papa, we build dat boat three time. Over and over. Ever year. Big work. Ever board, ever plank, ever rib, ever ting. Three time in forty year. We make dat to us. No papa, ees no-ting, just a rust. We make dat boat three time. My boat, Fader. I steal my boat.

"Da government say not my boat. What do you think, Fader, hey? I take dat boat. I steal da boat in da night, Fader."

"And you're very sorry."

"Yes-yes, *oui.*"

"Well, hmmm. Do you have any more sins since your last confession?"

"I don't think so, Fader. Not so bad. Not too many. Maybe drink too many whiskey. Some time. No harm. I don't fight, Fader. No-no. My papa, he say, Pierre, no fight. No fight. Not for me."

"Yes, my son. That's good. For your penance, say two Our Fathers and now an Act of Contrition, and we'll get you married here quite soon."

While I pray, I hear dis noise and shouting outside on da wharf.

"Amen, Fader."

"Bless you, son," he say.

I run up and dem bad guys from Fall Rivers got Rosa, and Sully he's lay out cold, and da bag guys got gun, point every where, all da crowd. Jeez. Big black cloud all da sky. I run down da wharf, screaming "Rosa, Rosa, my dear sweet Rosa, Rosa, Rosa."

All da people come. All da woman. All da kid. All da man. Come to see. Big lightening.

Da priest he hold my big gaf, pound the dock, bam, bam, bam, "Halt, sinners," he scream big voice. No sugar.

Thunder crack and boom. Sky flash white, den big crack.

"Bring me that girl!" da priest he yell. Boom. Pound da gaf. Bam, bam. "Halt."

All da people come dis way. Trap da bad guy.

"Rosa, Rosa! *Je t'aime. Je t'aime. Je t'aime*," to her yell I Pierre Louis and begin weep.

Big cheer from all da people. Push da bad guys. Hiss.

Lightening. Crack. Boom.

"Halt, sinners or die in hell!" yell da Priest. Red face. Very mad.

Den all hell break loose. Big flash. Hit da mast Mademoiselle Fleur, crack-aboom and dis white ball da light, I seen thees before me and papa, big ball we call dat St-Elmo fire dat ting, roll down da mast jump to the gaf hold to the priest, jump down da wharf, all the peoples they scream, and dat ball fire roll down da wharf and jump up da bad guys wid da gun, and des gun, dey crack and pop and smoke and dees bad boy dey drop da gun quick. One gun it fall in da water, sizzle and steam to bottom. Anoder fall on da wharf, hiss and burn and smoke and de bullet hiss and burn and pop.

Da bad boy burn da hands and shake dem ouch and run like hell.

"Go," shout da priest. "Repent, you sinners," he yell, big eyes, red face.

All da people stand back as da bad guy run up da wharf, up da Centre Street, up da Johnny Cake Hill, waving da hand like wing da bird.

All da peoples, dey cheer and clap da hand and come to da wedding, right der on da wharf, da priest he sugar again, say the word, bless Rosa, bless Pierre Louis, bless *Mademoiselle Fleur*, bless da peoples, bless da fleet, bless ever ting, drink da wine, all da peoples drink da wine, me and Rosa drink da wine.

Very good dis day. Happy end dis. Me and Rosa we sail away *Mademoiselle Fleur* big kees, many cheers all da peoples, wave goodbyes.

Harold Huber
Ottertail, MN

Seventy-fifth Birthday

Six AM: Woke up old
Five and seventy years
Antiqued, dinosaurian
Fossilistic

Seven AM: Not quite as old
Upright balance achieved
Hunger soothed, shaved, combed
Awaiting the postman

Eleven AM: Mailbox stuffed
Limericks and love notes
Tongue-in-cheek jabs
Methuselah jokes galore

Two PM: Hardly old at all
Write some lines, brisk walk
Joints and juices flowing
Bouncy step. Well, almost

Five PM: Snacked a bit
Napped A bit. Woke up
Dazed, out of sorts
Whined 'til I felt better

Eight PM: Neighbors call
(disrespectful mob)
"Stop fussing" "Here's a cake"
"Grow up, already!"

Nine PM: Stopped fussing
Ate cake, but that other
That "grow up," quite impossible
Tried so often

Eleven PM: Reviewed the day
Scanned the decades

Harold Huber

Searched for meanings. Found
Some sort-ofs. Gave it up

Tomorrow will be better
Birthday past, pressure off
Back-to-normal fretting
Down-to-earthish angst

Midnight hour: Time doth fly
Plump the pillow, close the eye
Sandman cometh. Beddy-bye
(Where's my mommy?)

* * *

O. C. Strunk
Calabash, NC 28467

Ode to the Smallmouth Bass

There are those who would think of you
as one of nature's creative survivors,
having traveled from the Midwest to Maine
without benefit of wagon train or keen-eyed scout.

And then there's the geek who once kept
dormitory lights on long past midnight,
his Ph.D. lips now addressing you confidently
as Micropterus dolomieu.

Of course, there are the barbarians
who see you only as a crusty brown slab
simmering over a camp fire
surrounded by wild carrots and blackened spuds.

O. C. Strunk

As for me, I think of you as
a freedom fighter, a patriot
whose fierce love of freedom sends you skyward
or propels you deep into a rocky heaven.

Even now, as I gently remove the wire
from your lips, you rest only briefly
before diving into a green world
where freedom awaits you–
a freedom I will never know and only imagine.

* * *

O. C. Strunk

Bird Talk

I would give this month's Social Security check
for a crash course in small bird language,
to understand the conversation going on
between the Carolina wren and the tufted titmouse
as they scratch atop the flat feeder
while I sip my twilight Merlot.

As it is, my anthroporphizing
has the titmouse complaining to the wren
for standing on a pine tuft–
three fresh needles it thinks
would make a neat back wall to the condo
it is building in my gazebo's rafters.

Or are they seriously chatting about
the tabby snoozing between the azalea bushes,
wondering if it is capable of a fifteen-foot dash
and an eight-foot leap? Undoubtedly, their parents

O. C. Strunk

warned them that cats can scale tall buildings
and are faster than a speeding locomotive.

There's even the possibility they're talking
about me, speculating if there might be
hiding between my head's two gray mounds
a mortar, or a grenade launcher,
or, more likely, a BB gun.

I consider this last notion pretty unfair
given that I am their benefactor.
No matter, for suddenly they take flight
in a swirl of sunflower seeds and millet,
their language now just another lost scroll.

As for me, I consider returning to my house.
I steal a glance at the remaining ounce of life
in my chalice and decide to stay at my post
until the last drop of wine has been drained
or until the language of wrens and titmice
seems unimportant, whichever comes first.

O. C. Strunk

Recollections

I am standing on the grass knoll
in the backyard looking out over the garden
at the giant black cherry tree
bordering the south end of the chicken yard.

It is fall and the garden stubble of onions,
carrots, tomato vines remain–
remnants of my adolescent sloth
and my father's long hours of railroading.

Lifting my eyes to scan beyond our acre,
the slate dumps loom like sleeping dinosaurs–
gray, silent, heavy, smothered by the ghosts
of a thousand dead workmen.

Behind me I hear the yapping of our fox terrier;
she is scratching the screen door,
wanting to join me, undoubtedly hoping I will
scratch a certain spot on the back of her neck.

What's strange about this view
is that grass knoll, garden remnants, cherry tree,
quarries, dog, and the thousand workmen
are but particles of settled dust.

At least that is what I am thinking
as a whiff of my mother's virgin bread
fills my nostrils and forms these words.

The Two Grandmas

by Kramer Greenfield.
Derry, New Hampshire

Grandmother: (n) the mother of one's mother or father. Grandma: a not-so-lean spoiling machine.

Grandmas exist to circumvent the straight line of discipline imposed on children by Mom, Dad, and other symbols of authority. They are adept at the kiss, hug, and spend; demonstrating unconditional acceptance to the recipient grandchild. Enter, from different stages; my best friend Maura's Mum, versus my Grandma.

Maura called her Grandma, Mum. Mum's face was a pale lily retaining grandeur, although wilted with age. Pale strawberry hair peeked under a round, tidy hat in perfect permed splendor. Her sharp blue eyes could look impassive, indignant, or nail you to the truth when a lie slipped halfway between your lips.

Mum drove a late model gray sedan. Her trim ankles in dainty strapped pumps, gingerly stepped from the car. She wore a fitted suit with lace or fur collar. A wire-hair terrier, Kappy, was tucked under one arm. The opposite hand grabbed her collar, touching the security of her pearls. Perhaps they were a reminder of her elevated station in life, or a mini life preserver keeping her afloat within the squalid setting. She disapproved of the entire housing projects with one sniff of the tilted nose. Mouth pursed in a hyphen of dismay, she searched. At the sight of Maura, the hyphen of her lip separated to allow a ray of smile to pass. She wiggled two gloved fingers in greeting.

Maura's mother announced to her father, "Your mother, (her royal highness?), has arrived."

My Grandma was Grandma, not so plain and not so simple. Her hair was rinsed a "gorgeous blue" arranged in a high bouffant. One blue curl rested on her forehead. Two others curled around her ears, like commas. Rhinestones imbedded the margins of her cataract glasses, magnifying the eyes to a fishbowl gleam. She was twice the size of Mum, wore sturdy lace-up shoes, and had no noticeable ankles at all. Necklace, earrings, and brooch were chosen for matching rhinestone brilliance to complement a vivid collection of flowered dresses. A puff of lavender was her signature, moving fragrantly with her shadow. Dad went to pick up Grandma in his old Studebaker car. She didn't mind being crowded there with three animated ragamuffin kids. Parked at the housing projects where we lived; her powdered and rouged cheeks smiled in beaming anticipation. All her grandbabies bustled through the door hollering, "Grandma's here! Grandma's here!"

My mother grumbled under her breath, "the old battle axe", but attempted to hug the huge circumference of Grandma's waist. They kissed the air next to each other's cheek for a greeting.

It didn't seem possible to hug Mum without breaking something delicate. If you achieved an actual hug, she moaned about wrinkling her clothes. My Grandma, on the other hand, was a wide bodied hug machine, whose enthusiastic efforts nestled you into her garden bosom until it became difficult to breathe. Mum hugged Maura carefully and completely, maybe thinking, "Well, now, that's over and done."

Maura's strawberry hair and blue eyes amazed Mum. They reflected rainbows of resemblance, recalling her long forgotten youth. Mum wore widowhood like a badge of dignity, and was very comfortable with being alone, thank you. Then Maura came along to shake her perfectly arranged world in a quite unexpected, but not unwelcome fashion.

If you yelled, "Hi! Grandma!" to her, she winced at the offense. Usually, she waved her two fingered gloved salute for greeting, to dismiss you ever so polite. I thought she was sort of a Grandma, but not full fledged Grandma material. I pictured her on *What's My Line?* the TV quiz show, as everyone tried to guess her occupation. She would stump the panel before she finally admitted to being a Grandma.

Mum walked away with Maura in one gloved hand, and her annoying, barking dog still tucked under her arm. Maura was whisked away in the sedan to the never-never land of Mum's house for a weekend. I watched them drive away wondering if the woman knew what to do with a little kid. I always worried myself sick until Maura returned unscathed and unbitten.

Maura looked suspiciously at my Grandma, a big exaggerated version of her Mum. Her eyes widened at the vision of Grandma's walking smorgasbord of color and sparkle. Grandma's blue hair was once golden brown, although more neatly controlled than my unruly mop. Behind the thick glasses, her brown eyes twinkled and echoed mine. Even with the vague resemblance, Maura considered her a Grandma overdose. When she bent down to pat her head, Maura freaked out. It was too much Grandma for her to handle.

Grandma was my father's mother, but she and Ma both loved control. Each strived to be "Boss," in Dad's house. Grandma hated being alone, so joined us for Sunday dinner every week; where she and Ma fought for prime time. Sometimes when Maura came over, they were hollering to the tune of clapping pans, creating the pandemonium of the Battle of Bunker Hill. Maura asked if they were fighting? "Nah, I'd say, that's how they talk to each other." All the noise was matter of fact to me, but Maura's mother and Mum hardly spoke at all. They talked in hushed lady-like tones.

Often Grandma took me by the hand, guiding me possessively to Dad's car to be driven to her house for a couple of days. Maura probably thought I was going to the land of Oz, where the wizard was a domineering female monster who may or may not help me find the way home. She looked worried when I waved and made funny faces to her from the Studebaker's rear view window.

Because Maura and I were best friends, it was inevitable these two parallels meet in a neutral zone. Maura's Mum was already aware of our gang of kids and animals. Ma stood on the back step, yelling embarrassingly loud, "So Hello Mrs. G! (Mum) Yoo-Hoo, Hello!". Giving credit where it was due, Mum waved her whole gloved hand and opened her mouth to respond; but no words came out. Maybe Mum thought Ma some birth giving heathen to be reluctantly admired, but whatever did one say to her?

My Grandmother and Ma were all about noise and speaking your mind. They passionately grabbed their share of fruit from the tree of life. They were fiercely protective, never ashamed of grand displays of affection. Maura's mother and Mum were about keeping up appearances and doing what was expected of you. They walked a catwalk of possessions and measured out affection by the thimble.

You can imagine how my horror collided with Mum's when Maura decided to pull the elegant Mrs. G. over to our porch, where Ma and Grandma sat like two overfed tigresses in stressed lounge chairs.

My Grandma wore a corset under her dress with a network of "bones" complex enough to erect a portion of the Mystic River Bridge. This situation forced Grandma to lean backward as she sat, producing no visible lap whatsoever. My Mother had enough lap for both of them, tending to lean her bulk forward. They talked non-stop, often interrupting each other without apology. Oh no, I worried, what do the two Grandmas have in common? What will they talk about? How will I keep Ma from constant interruption? I was frantic.

"This is my Mum," said Maura. She was proud to show off her Grandma, who automatically turned rigid with self control.

"How DO you DO?" Mum said, but I figured she was planning a quick escape. Maybe she thought of murdering my best friend. Ma and Grandma,

Tweedle Dee and Tweedle Dum, were all social smiles, complete with compliments.

"I see where Maura gets her lovely red hair", said Grandma. Mum jumped when Ma leaped from the chair to rescue my baby brother, who ventured too close to the main street. Ma was fat, but fast on her feet. Grandma continued, "We are so lucky to have such beautiful granddaughters!"

Maura and I looked at each other. Only a Grandma believed you beautiful when your teeth were stepstools, and your hair was overpermed and undercombed. Maura's Mum looked surprised. Maybe she suspected Grandma might bark like the terrier, or the many rhinestones she wore might be contagious. Grandma was hefty, and did not assume correct posture sitting in the chair, but her heart was firmly in the right place. They gave each other a Grandma look. The look reserved for the unannounced joy derived from the mere presence of the little girls standing before them. We continued their history, and became the future. Love lived in each circle of arms that surrounded us. Maura and I stole a glance at each other. So the two Grandmas were not so different at all.

But then Ma returned, and the ice cream man rang his bell. My Mother and Grandma reached deeply into their respective bosoms for money. I thought Mum might fall into a dead faint, so Maura and I stood on either side of the old gal for support. We led her away from my darling barbarians to a Queen Anne chair at Maura's project apartment to recuperate.

We made her strong tea served in a delicate china cup. Well, of course, there were still a few differences, but Maura and I thought it went quite well under the circumstances.

Breach of Security

Bette Anderson
Laguna Beach, CA

Monday at the Library:

Noises from the children's wing slowly intruded into Kathy's consciousness. Two young boys were sharing a book, open to what she suspected was smuggled adult material, and erupting frequently with high-pitched laughter. She really didn't want to know what they were up to, but they were beginning to disturb other library users, so she walked over to them.

"Hi, boys," she said softly. "Having a good time?"

They looked up distrustfully. One of them closed the book and held it behind his back.

"We ain't doin' nothin', Miss."

"Of course you're not," she said, keeping her voice low and friendly. "It's just that you're a little noisy. Can you quiet down a bit?"

"Yes, Ma'am," they said in unison.

Kathy left them, sensing their relief that she hadn't seized their reading material. She figured they'd been dumped in the library after school while their mothers went shopping. Baby-sitting went with the territory. But overall Kathy loved the library, with its walls of books, humming computers and microfiche readers, all providing multiple paths to knowledge. There was nothing she liked better than searching for answers to hard questions.

When Kathy next looked for them the boys were gone. Probably hiding amid the Harry Potter books, she thought, smiling.

The afternoon wore on. White-haired Mr. Jorgenson, a veteran library user now in his 90's, fell asleep in his chair with the *The Atlantic* open on his lap. Kathy or Sue, the other librarian on duty, would awaken him at closing time.

Roger Amster, who ran a local delivery service for groceries ordered off the Internet, stopped by. As usual, he cornered Sue and launched into a long story obviously intended to impress her with his acumen in the world of food commerce. It took five minutes for her to disentangle herself.

Kathy, meanwhile, found her attention drawn to another part of the room, furnished with lounge chairs and low reading lamps, currently unoccupied except for two men in adjacent seats. They were talking quietly. Accustomed to the informal dress and mannerisms of the usual library patrons, Kathy found their appearance odd. They wore dark suits and ties and shiny shoes--like movie gangsters, she thought, almost giggling at the thought. She stopped herself just in time as she walked in their direction, heading for the copy machine.

Just as she came within earshot one of them looked up and saw her. Both immediately rose and moved to the nearest book stack, the short story collection, where they appeared to be fascinated by the titles.

She shrugged and continued on.

On Mondays the library closed early, so at 5:45 Kathy and Sue began "closing procedures," shutting down the machines and turning off the main lights.

"Did you notice the black suits?" asked Kathy, still curious.

Sue laughed. "Oh yes. Conspicuous in their finery. What's your best guess?"

"Mafia, maybe?"

"Wrong. They're some kind of officials, I'm sure. I saw them earlier in our director's office, huddling over circulation records. They're allowed access under the Patriot Act, you know. If they ask, we have to give them the titles of books people are reading."

"Bummer," said Kathy. "Why doesn't Alison fight it?"

"She really can't," said Sue. "It's a no-winner. If she doesn't comply with the law she loses her job."

"I suppose so. Should we talk to her about it? Tell her we'll support her if she takes a stand?"

Sue shook her head. "That would just get us all fired. No, there's nothing we can do."

"Do you have any idea who the men are after?" asked Kathy.

Sue lowered her voice to a whisper. "Scuttlebut says it's one of our favorite customers, Randy Taxil."

Kathy was surprised. "Randy? Why him? He's totally harmless."

"I know what you mean," said Sue, visualizing the boy—he could hardly be more than 20—with his dark hair and pale, ascetic face. Randy often came to the library to search out esoteric subjects on the Internet, occasionally asking for help from the librarians. Confused by the Dewey Decimal System, he sometimes had difficulty locating books. "He's always polite and self-effacing. Sweet is the word, if it applies to men."

"What's his nationality?" asked Kathy.

"The name Randy sounds English, but Taxil could be Arab-American.

There's

something old-worldly about him, don't you think? He's too courteous to be German or French, and his speech is too formal for him to be a native-born American. He sounds as if he only recently learned the language."

Kathy laughed. "Maybe he's a Saudi prince in disguise."

"Careful—you'll be accused of profiling."

"Tell you what. Just for fun, let's call up his file and see what he's into."

Sue laughed. "I'm way ahead of you. The *Norton Anthology of Literature, European Art, Basic Chemistry,* to name just a few."

"Eclectic but hardly incriminating. I wonder why the Feds are interested."

"No idea," said Sue. "We'll just have to wait and see."

Tuesday: Randy Meets His Accusers:

Randy Taxil sat stiffly in a library study carrel pretending to read the lead story, about another London bombing attempt, of *The New York Times.* His eyes were fixed on the type but not moving. Accustomed to being the object of scrutiny, he'd noticed the surreptitious glances of two formally dressed men nearby. He had an uneasy feeling he was a target. In a case of mistaken identity, he'd once been falsely arrested and held overnight in jail, an experience that left him with profound disgust and fear of authority.

His peripheral vision caught a moving image of a middle-aged woman in a gray suit. Suddenly she was standing beside him.

"Mr. Taxil," she said in a soft but clearly modulated voice, "I'm Alison Whittier, the Library Director. Could I ask you to step into my office for a minute?"

He looked up. The two men had moved toward her and were now at her side.

"May I please to ask what for?" he asked.

"Of course," said Alison. "These men are from the federal government, and they would like to ask you a few questions—nothing to be concerned about, just a matter of checking some records."

Randy was still suspicious of the dark pair and didn't trust the director either, but felt he had no choice but to comply. "I am presently engaged in extensive literary research," he said, rising. "I trust this will not take long. But since you asked so graciously for a few moments of my time I shall be happy to provide them."

Alison Whittier smiled, as did both men—evilly, it seemed to Randy. The four of them walked into the director's office.

"Please have a seat," she said. "Would anyone like coffee? I keep a fresh pot on hand." She motioned toward a small table on which rested an urn and several coffee mugs. Randy's perfect vision made it possible for him to read their lettering:

"Be All You Can Be—Use Your Library."

"Yes, please," he said politely.

"Cream and sugar?"

"No thank you."

The agents declined. In the silence that ensued as Alison poured the coffee Randy's anxiety grew.

Finally she spoke. "I need to tell you, Mr. Taxil, that I have given these men some information on your library usage, plus a list of ten books you have recently checked out. I might add that this is not a task I relish, but they are legally entitled to the information. I hope you will understand."

With a shock Randy realized he was actually being investigated by the U.S. Government. But they can't put me in jail for reading books, he thought. What else do they know? Suddenly he had a feeling of transparency, as it they could see everything about him—his Middle Eastern family, the amount in his bank account, his ambitions, his secret desires.

"Is that all?" he asked, trying to remain calm. When there was no immediate reply he stood up. "I must get back to my work."

"And what might that be?" asked one of the men. "Sit down, Taxil. We're not through with you yet."

For the next hour Randy underwent in-depth questioning regarding his background (in the U.S. on a student visa, currently pursuing a degree at the local college), frequency of library visits (two or three times a week), main interests (literature and art) and personal contacts. Here he demurred, mistakenly believing there was no way the men could discover the identities of his friends.

"We already have your phone records," they told him. "It would just speed things up if you give us some names."

So this is what it means to have your privacy violated, Randy thought. He shook his head sadly. "I can't believe this is happening in America."

The taller of the men looked annoyed. "You better believe it. Since 9/11 we don't fool around with terrorists. You can go now, but bear in mind we'll be watching you."

Wednesday: Balancing Liberty and Security:

The interrogators had names: Gary Norman, former private investigator employed by the FBI since 1998, and Craig Berger, a ten-year espionage veteran and Gary's immediate supervisor. They'd been assigned to Randy's case after an anonymous phone call had alerted the Bureau to a possible, albeit tenuous, connection between a young Muslim named Randi, or Randy, and a London extremist network. They had traced the call and learned it was from an estranged girlfriend of Randy Taxil. When they interviewed her she mentioned the name of a known terrorist and claimed that Randy knew him. Despite a thorough check the agents could find no evidence of contact between the two. They decided to tighten their surveillance.

"He's as guilty as they come," said Gary.

"Absolutely," agreed Craig. "A terrorist if I ever saw one. Here's the plan. We check with the library to see what he's been reading, get a Patriot Act warrant to search his apartment, then put a tail on him and bug his phone. He must have accomplices."

By subjecting Randy's phone records to minute scrutiny the agents managed to identify two of his acquaintances, one of whom was a Pakistani who had been in London at the same time as Randy and the other a young art teacher he had met at a MOMA exhibit. Her background was strictly American heartland, so the agents concluded that she knew nothing. "My guess is that it's just sex," snorted Gary.

The Pakistani seemed a more likely suspect, but even in his case evidence of a terrorist connection was elusive, although Gary and Craig were convinced it was there. They continued to hover in the shadows, causing Randy to become more and more agitated. He booked a flight to London, where he thought he would be safe. It was a serious mistake.

Thursday: Idle Conversations:

It was a quiet afternoon. Kathy leafed through Booklist, searching for titles to add to the collection, and Sue skimmed the contents of a pamphlet she'd picked up from a shelving cart. "This is more than I ever wanted to know about food additives," she said.

"Me too," said Kathy. "Scary stuff, isn't it? Makes you almost want to stop eating."

"I wouldn't go that far," said Sue, whose somewhat voluptuous figure testified to her love of food. "But speaking of dieting, have you noticed how thin and pale our little friend Randy looks lately?"

Kathy considered. "Yes, and I'm worried about him. Maybe the stress of this investigation is too much for him to handle. Do you know if he has a lawyer?"

"I don't think so. Alison said she suggested it, but he said he didn't have the money."

"Poor boy. What's going to happen to him?"

"I suppose it all depends on whether he's guilty or not," said Sue.

Kathy rolled her eyes. "Of what? Reading too many books? Not being an American citizen?"

"No, but—" Sue hesitated. "Those agents—they must have something on him or they'd let him alone. They can't just make things up."

"I think they can and do. Look up Homeland Security on the Internet. You'll be surprised at the powers they have."

"Well, maybe. . ." said Sue, still doubtful. Just then, Roger Amster appeared, armed with samples from his truck, and it was several minutes before the librarians could gracefully decline his gifts and steer him into another area. The day ended without further incident.

Friday:Best-Laid Plans:

Randy arrived at the airport early for his flight, allowing more than the suggested two hours, and waited patiently in the long security line. In a "might as well spend it" mood he had raided his tuition money to book a seat in business class, and planned to spend the extra time in the Elite Lounge until it was time to board the plane.

But no sooner had he settled down with a cup of coffee than the federal agents appeared. "I'm afraid," said Craig, "that you won't be able to finish that. You have to come with us."

Randy drew back, startled and fearful. "Why? What have I done?"

"You're wanted for questioning on a matter of national security."

"What do you mean? "

"You tell us," said Gary. "We've just learned of another plot to bomb a London subway—and you just happen to be going there. Not today, not tomorrow, my boy. Our chief wants to talk to you. You have a lot of questions to answer, Randy Taxil."

Two Years Later:

A new expansion program has been announced for the library, supported in part by federal funds. Alison Whittier has been commended by the government for her cooperation and given a raise. Kathy and Sue are still fielding reference questions and passes from patrons. Sue has a new admirer—Hans Reid, a stockbroker she met in the business section—and Kathy is working on a doctorate in library science. She hopes to go on to bigger and better assignments, although she's not yet sure what they might be. Mr. Jorgenson goes to sleep for the last time. The librarians attend his funeral.

"Attention must be paid," says Kathy, borrowing a line from ***Death of a Salesman.***

Randy Taxil is still incarcerated as a "security risk," pursuant to provisions of the Patriot Act and a continuing national climate of fear. He has repeatedly denied any connection with terrorists. He says that his education was financed by his mother and her British husband, not Islamic support groups, and certainly not Al Quaeda. No charges have been filed and no date set for trial.

But there has been one change. Randy has a lawyer, a civil rights activist with a successful court record. Anonymous sources are paying for his services.

To show their support, the library staff sends Randy a handmade Hurry-Back-We've-Missed-You card and cancels all of his late fees.

Margaret Bobalek King
East Derry, NH

Angels' Pursuit Of The Water Sign

If you try to be a wave
we will be the foam.
If you try to hide under still waters
beneath the placid, stagnant, tropical sea
we will be deep spokes of a relentless sun
flashing through sea-dazzle.

If you try to hide in coastal waters
in murky Florida swamps
we will be the mangrove roots
choking you off. If you go inland
and find refuge in freshwater ponds
we will thicken you with blooms
of green algae creeping on your bare breast.
Our hot air vapors rising skyward
will be our loving incense.

If you try to run from us
helter-skeltering down hills
leaping rocks and logs, a brook in a hurry
we will be waiting for you in deep, silent pools
by the beaversdam where the trout watch.
If you try to evade us
through chinks in the cut trees
we will soak you up with cedar roots.

You cannot hide from us
neither in salt water nor in fresh
not in swift-running streams
nor when the deep stirs or is still.
We will lie in wait for you
Water Sign, and lift you
trembling and moist
on our winged hands and carry you
in restless air to your secret source.

Margaret Bobalek King

Pan's Song

He sang to me and played
on the harp of high winds
herding the sheep in blue heaven.
He sang in the riot of candy colors
in my garden, pulsing with passion
in purple petunias, blowing the brassy
horn's blast of marigolds, curling the
subtle petals of the Peace Rose.

He sang in nasturtiums bitter
as radishes, in pungent lettuces
gone to seed, in bridal white
of pure gladiolus. He whispered
a wind's breath through rustling
aspens, whistling a thousand
choruses, tossing scatters
of sunlight to his song.

He sang in the rustle of grass
thirsty for rain that pricked my arm
as I rested ear on elbow, close to clover
listening to screeching violins
in the dim heat of summer, Vivaldi's cicadas.
Their reason for being is love
and their love is better than mine
for they sing, find fulfillment and die.

Like him they sing! Like him
their terrible song is of love
and their love is better than mine.
I lie in the grass shouting "Peace!"
Take your song that goes on and on
that gives me no rest, that pierces
me to the breast. Teach me that fierce melody!
For I have so little time left to sing.

The Fiftieth
By John Cannon
San Diego, CA

I might have walked right past the cab, except that it was so clean and perfect that I stopped to admire it. On my street, there aren't any cabs. It's a CTA kind of neighborhood, and people take the bus, or maybe the El. Me, I'm a bus girl. Five days a week to Home Depot, where I work in the plumbing department. Copper pipe, shower fixtures, irrigation stuff. I know it all, so go ahead and ask me, I won't bite your head off.

So, this Yellow Cab. Not a swipe of grime, no greasy smears, no thick layer of brake dust on the front wheels of this hack. No dings in the fenders, not even any streaks on the windows. It glowed golden at the curb. I could see inside, and it was preposterously immaculate. It could never have hauled anyone home from the Booze N Beef on Devon Avenue at 2 in the morning. The driver, or at least the man of indeterminate age who held the rear door open, beamed incandescence. His clothing was flawless, and I stared. All right, already, so I was gawking at him. The black suit of traditional cut and the white shirt. The cufflinks and the club tie. The shoes polished so rigorously that the glare hurt my eyes. And the bowler, the likes of which I had never seen in real life on a real head.

"Good morning, Ms. Truhardt." The caramel words came from beneath the bowler. Something is clearly out of whack here.

He appeared to be talking to me.

"Ms. Truhardt?" I said. "Well, don't you have the manners. And how do you know my name?"

His round face, a gently sloping landscape marked by cheeky hillocks of flesh, broke into another smile.

"But Ms. Molly Truhardt, it's your birthday, and of course I know who you are," he said, maintaining good posture and radar-lock eye contact.

Now I'm worried. This guy knew my name, my birthday. But he was so polite.

"You simply must take a ride."

"Why simply must I? I take the bus every day and who knows who the hell you are." I prepared to walk toward the Chicago Transit Authority stop.

A sigh escaped him. He looked almost hurt. Damn, I hate when they look hurt.

"Believe me," he said, "This is cheaper than the bus and infinitely more entertaining."

More entertaining than the CTA? DON'T MAKE ME LAUGH! Here is a man too long separated from public transit and its clientele: the poor, the young, and the criminally insane. But yeah, I got in. Oh, don't give me that. I know it was about the last thing I should have done. But it was my 50th birthday and can you blame me for looking for adventure or romance or something impossible in my life? Of course you can't, so shut up and listen.

I knew I would be safe. It was the guy's face. And this cab was no creaking, battered Crown Vic or Impala. This was a cut above. This was a Checker, the roomy, bulbous make that I always associated with taxi cabs, although I hadn't seen one since the '70s. I sat back as Bowler closed the door, which shut with a satisfying whump, nothing like the blang of the '86 Subaru I had before it was totaled on the Kennedy when that idiot in the Dodge minivan swerved into me. The guy told the cops that he had been trying to take a picture of downtown Chicago on his cell phone and send it to his mother in Cedar Rapids. The cab interior smelled like the Porsche I sat in at the auto show once. There was absolutely no evidence that this was an actual Yellow Cab. Like I said, there wasn't the slightest trace of puke in the back seat.

"Well, here we are," the driver said in a voice that rounded the vowels.

"Here we are where?" I shot back with my best city attitude. People told me my voice was full of Chicago. I had no idea what they meant. "We've been in the cab 30 seconds. You just put the thing in gear, for God's sake. We're not at the Home Depot."

I almost wanted to be at Home Depot. It wasn't such a bad place, especially in comparison to being in a cab with a crackpot. It was kind of fun to embarrass those thumby men who didn't know what male and female pipe fittings were. And besides, it was easy work that let me spend the rest of my time trying to start my own architecture firm. All in all, it was better than the 20 years I spent as an office manager. So there.

"Ms. Truhardt, it's your fiftieth birthday, correct?"

Really, how did he know?

"Actually, I'm glad you don't know what's about to happen. It means the secret yet holds. The Fellowship of the Fiftieth is intact."

"Would you mind?" I asked. "You're not making a lot of sense and I'm getting out of this cab right now."

"Absolutely, Ms. Truhardt. It is time for you to get out."

The cab was stopped. The rear door was open, somehow, and I could see we were still in Rogers Park, my homey lakefront neighborhood. I've always been the curious type.

"So whaddaya mean this is what happens on your fiftieth birthday? What's all that fellowship stuff?"

Puffy cheeks rose toward the hat, propelled north by his smile.

"You see Ms. Truhardt, we all disappear for a little while on our fiftieth birthday. It's a gift from . . . well, from the person who controls these things. You have a short while to visit any time in your life. Nearly everyone chooses the past. Oh, some do make a trip to the future, but the percentage is infinitesimal."

I laughed a loud, snorting, head-clearing laugh. Finally, it came together. This whole thing was the work of Brian in Floor Coverings. Honestly, the guy was such a joker, always with the wisecrack. He must have found out that it was my birthday. Probably from Donna in Outdoor Garden, who is such a blabbermouth. How the hell will I ever get back at them? As I wiped my eyes, I chanced a look out the open door of the cab. The man passing by strutted in platform shoes, wide belt and shirt open to mid chest. He was sheathed in polyester. His blown-dry hair fit his head like a cap. None of this registered. I caught a look at the news rack chained to the nearby street light and the big Tribune headline said something about Mayor Bilandic.

I wheeled around to face Bowler again, perched a little forward now on the cab's back seat.

"Now, wait a minute . . ."

"Yes, Ms. Truhardt, it's 1977 for you. This is the gift known to the initiated as The Fiftieth. You're going to revisit a part of your past. All the usual time travel rules apply, of course. It goes without saying that you can't go back and kill your own grandfather or anything like that, and the rules about whether you actually see your past self are so complicated I don't want to even get into it, so let's just leave that alone, OK? You just get to visit, and then you are sworn to secrecy. You can't mention this to anyone 49 or younger."

My mouth was starting to dry out. It had been hanging open too long.

"You're kidding me, right? Brian didn't put you up to this? This is insane. Maybe it's that Thai food I had last night."

"No, dear. I don't even know Brian that well. He's only in his 30s. This happens to everyone on their fiftieth. Not always a cab, of course, but our research indicated it would work on you. Now your friend Giselle, the one who wants to live in Florence, we plan to send a young man on a Vespa to her condo when the time is right."

Strange feelings roiled my brain.

"This happens to everyone? And no one tells?"

"That is how it has worked."

"For how long?"

"A very long time"

"How long?"

"Really, Ms. Truhardt, it doesn't matter. No one tells. It's the one thing mankind agrees upon. Oh, some people come close to divulging, and some people get stuck in their favorite time period and don't fully disengage. Like Dick Clark."

I could see that.

"So, Ms. Truhardt, here you are in 1977, which our research indicated you had an interest in visiting. Your college graduation year and such. But really, 1977? Never would have been my choice. And, by the way, this all goes relatively quickly. There's no set time period. It just ends. That's part of the fun! So, I'm off, but I won't be far. Follow the rules, or . . ."

"Or what?"

"Let's just keep this happy, shall we? There are Bee-Gees to listen to, Sylvester Stallone movies to see and perhaps old friends you may want to check on."

I guess I got that faraway look.

"So, Ms. Truhardt, no destruction of the time-space continuum is allowed. What happened in the past stays in the past. In that way, the Fiftieth is a bit like Las Vegas. No changing things, no investing in about-to-boom neighborhoods, yadda yadda. Oh, I'm sorry, I've had some trips lately to the '90s and I keep seeing that Seinfeld episode where they do that."

"Can I get out now?" I asked. My head had cleared and I was so curious about where I was and what was happening that I could have erupted.

"Why, yes, of course."

I was in Rogers Park. I think. The light was different. The feel was off. I was momentarily nauseous, and then things snapped into place again. The cab was gone, and I was standing on the street. The window of Rosen's Bakery showed my reflection. I blanched. My hair was curly and shaped into what can only be described as an afro. I had on short cutoff jeans, and I mean short. I grabbed a paper out of the machine, intending to learn about Mayor Bilandic, and reached for my reading glasses to see the small print that these newspaper editors insist upon. But wait, I'm reading the paper without glasses. I'm not squinting and I'm not vainly searching for the right distance to hold the paper. I can see, dammit! But the 'fro, jeez, did I ever look like that? Part of this Fiftieth deal is that you get your body from your favorite time in the past?

The streets are full of Datsun B-210s and rusty Oldsmobile Cutlasses. It might really be 1977. It was mid-afternoon, and on my birthday in 1977 I had a test in that Modern American Novels class. I remember because I was so woefully unprepared then I almost made myself sick. I spied a clock on the wall of a barber shop, the proprietor of which had not yet evolved into a stylist, and I saw that I had enough time to get to the class at Loyola. I hiked over to Damen Hall and rode up the escalators to the sixth floor and slipped into the nondescript classroom just as things were about to start. The time warp really smacked me in the noggin then – a classroom full of people dressed in full 1977. Post-hippie, peri-disco. Professor Clayton (he hadn't changed a bit; wait, of course he hadn't) handed out the blue books. I was looking forward to this. Words of warning sounded in my head repeatedly, like the recorded announcement in the Midway Airport concourses that advises people the moving walkway was ending. You can't change what happened in the past. Yeah, yeah, I know all about it. But where's the harm if I ace this test? I'm so much smarter now than I was in college. So, if I ace the test, I get an A in the class overall, it raises my GPA just enough to let me graduate cum laude, because I was right on the cusp back then and it's always been a sore spot with me. That wouldn't really be messing with the past, would it? Can you believe it, I glanced at the door as the professor closed it and caught a glimpse of a bowler and the expression on the face below it fairly shouted: Don't disappoint me, Ms. Truhardt. I hesitated when I got the test and saw the question that asked me to compare and contrast the central themes in the works of Bernard Malamud to those of Philip Roth. But just for a second. Please don't let me run out of ink.

After class, I walked north, to soak in the sights of Rogers Park as I remembered it. When I passed the funky clothes shop on Sheridan Road north of Albion, I remembered that some of the basketball players had heard that the place was really a front for a bookie. Maybe they were right, because I never once saw anyone buying clothes in there. I'm going in. I have an idea. It might loosen the intricate weave of the fabric of time, but how many shots do you get at something like this? What, me worry?

I strolled in and was taken aback by the scent of patchouli oil. T-shirts were deployed haphazardly on rickety tables and display racks. The guy I figured to be the owner, he of the frizzy fading hair and well-tended fu manchu mustache, reclined languidly in a rattan chair toward the rear of the overly warm storefront. He seemed not to mind at all that a papyrus-like sale sign was peeling off the side wall.

"Hi, babe, need some help?"

Babe? Good God, this is a time warp.

"Uh, that depends. I've heard some things about this place and I wonder if they're true."

"That depends."

"On what?"

"On what you heard." His smile revealed a missing incisor. I bit back a weird mix of revulsion and desire to howl like a hyena in his face.

"Well, I heard, you know, that people could make a bet here."

The smile disappeared and his features set up like cement on a hot afternoon.

"You a cop?"

"I look like a cop?" I cocked one hip and placed a hand on it. I can play the saucy tart if need be.

His eyes danced about my body, overly long, I thought, if he's trying to figure if I have a badge and gun hidden somewhere in these tight clothes.

"OK, guess you're a student. I've seen you walk past the shop millions of times anyway with your books and all."

Without saying more, I followed his gaze to a back door. I walked toward it slowly, gave it a shove and belatedly wondered whether I had any money.

"Hello, young lady, how may I be of service?" A geezer in a seersucker jacket peered at me over the top of plastic-framed glasses, the kind that turned white when they got old or got too sweaty too many times. His were really white. In that airless room, smoke streamed straight toward the ceiling from the fat cigar in the pressed-metal ashtray near his right hand.

"Well," I said, affecting the tough-broad manner that I thought would work best, "I'd like to make a bet on the horses."

"Horses?"

I resisted the urge to say, yes, tall animals with four legs that run fast. Instead, I nodded.

"How much would you like to bet, and on which horse?"

"I'd like to make a special bet if it's allowed. I'd like to bet on a horse to win the Triple Crown."

Bushy eyebrows raised a notch. I knew he was appraising the fine catch I would make as soon as he set the hook. I let him think that.

"As you wish. The odds are pretty high though."

"Oh, I know. Here's $100," I said. It was in my pocket. Bowler was daring me to spend it.

"Which horse?" he asked.

"Oh," I said, giving my head a little turn so that the blonde fro bounced. "I have a really good feeling. Put it on Seattle Slew."

Knowledge is good.

The sun was beginning to settle. A Friday evening and here I was in Rogers Park in 1977. I knew where I needed to go before time ran out. So I began the five-block walk. I made my way south on Sheridan Road and crossed Devon. A block on and there it was – Monroe's. No matter what year you see it, I guess, it always looks the same. There was that time in the '80s when some new owners tried to clean it and the place veered dangerously close to fern bar, but that was then. Or it would be then. Or is it now? I don't know.

I took a deep breath and walked in.

"There you are," he said. He was at the bar and turned when I came in, taking a break from making rings on the bar with the condensation from his beer glass.

Damn. There he was. Matt of the Hundred Days. That's how I later came to think of him, because it described how long we were together. We'd loved so intensely that I often wondered whether we'd consumed each other.

"Hi, Matt." It sounded so strange to say it, to see him. He doesn't know that I haven't seen him or talked to him for more than 25 years. He thinks he saw me this morning in class, where we made plans to meet here. I'm sweating, spinning, feeling like an observer of my own life. Should I leave, is my time up yet?

He touches my shoulder and then the back of my neck. I'll stay.

"Happy birthday, again," he says, looking at me with those eyes. "Ready to come to my place so you can get your present?"

His place. We walked out of the tavern, hand-in-hand, headed toward Matt's apartment on Kenmore. On the walk, I remembered that Matt was almost two years older than me. I wonder what he did on his fiftieth? I bet he'd be the type who went forward. No matter. We had arrived at his gloomy studio in one of those abominable four-plus-one apartment buildings they built all over the city in the '60s and '70s. Only two small windows in Matt's place, and paint was peeling from their frames at a furious pace. I'd never noticed before. Apartments and houses and accumulated stuff meant less to me then, because no one I knew then had much stuff. In the little apartment, the Goodwill table was set with mismatched plates and silverware, but the scent from the oven was thick and rich, and a candle Matt had just lit painted us both in amber.

"I made lasagna. I have this Chianti," he said. Of course, I knew that, I had drunk it in 1977. A very fine year. What about the time, I wondered. Bowler said a short while, but couldn't that mean a few days? What happens at the end? Would Bowler suddenly appear at the door? I didn't care to find out. I was going to make this count.

"You're beautiful, Molly, and I love you," he said to me. The scent, the light, the feeling roaring through me.

The kiss was gentle at first, and then, well, our embraces always tended toward the passionate.

Our lips parted briefly. We needed to breathe – mere details.

"Some people would call a kiss like that electric," he said.

"Would you?" I asked him.

"No, I'd say that was nuclear."

Simply said, there was no separating us. I worked my arms around his shoulders. He worked his around my waist. My hands went to the sides of his face. The top button of my shirt was undone. Then the next. Matt worked his way down the row, and I did the same on his blue Western shirt. It was 1977, nearly the beginning of that pathetic Urban Cowboy phase, but we were always ahead of the trends. Shirts off, the lush sensation of skin on skin. He touched the hollow of my back. His breath in my ear, his hands on my hips, and then my ribs. My lips on his neck, his hands softly finding their way to my breasts. A satin caress. A May breeze could not have been as gentle. God, the sheer joy of it.

"Is this the present?" I asked. I wasn't sure whether I had said it out loud.

"Well, no, but it could be," said Matt of the Hundred Days.

"The present is over there." He looked toward a rickety end table.

A vase. Red roses, all thorns painstakingly removed by a florist, in the old way. I'm melting. We wrapped each other in our arms.

I'm in that place where nothing in the world matters but my lover, where our embrace is the universe, where our kiss connects us so absolutely that we nearly become each other. Being experienced and young simultaneously, I want to lock Matt and his hands and face into me forever.

Quick breaths, tingling and electric. I'm beyond the reach of earth, I'm... in the back seat of a cab?

"Ms. Truhardt?" a voice says. It is vaguely familiar. I fight making the connection.

"Are you back with us?" the voice says.

"YOU? I'm in this stupid cab?" I was spitting words at him. "Do you know where I was? Do you have any idea what you just interrupted? What kind of crap is this?"

"Now Ms. Truhardt, the time was up. Many people have told me that this is an annoying part of the present, but there is no predicting when the present ends."

"You mean present as in now, or present as in gift?"

"Well, both, my dear. Time is such an odd concept."

I looked at where I was. We were driving down Sheridan, back to my condo. The cab pulled to a stop behind the hybrid Honda that my neighbor parked in front of our building. Back to the future.

I got out. I was physically spent, but it seemed as if every sense was open only to good stuff. The spray of lilac blooms in the yard, delicate Chopin drifted gently from a living room down the street. I even smiled at that skanky young skateboarder who lived in the brick bungalow next door, the one whose passage is marked by a trail of well-smoked Kools. I hadn't felt like this since, well, when? Since that way-back-when time.

"I'm so alive!" I said to the skateboarder. I said it quite loudly.

As I walked slowly up the sidewalk, I reached for my key and found a piece of paper in my pants pocket. The betting ticket. Could there be interest? I practically bounced up the stairs to my place.

That may be why I didn't see it right away. The single red rose outside my door. The one with the smooth stem.

No thorns.

Rose Kabat
Laguna Hills, CA

Longing

I move with
the motion of morning
feel the beat of
    my heart
A strong wind
rises, small stones
sprout wings and
    fly
Branches of hemlock
sift the sun
all is a scattering
    a shining
I pass the graveyard
where white crosses
in permanent quiet
    march
in single file
converge at a point
somewhere on
    the horizon
The sky
turns scarlet
the color of
    wounds
the shredded
fabric of
wartime
    memories
I rock with
the motion
of morning
    long
for a peace
that lasts as
long as life
    endures

The Six Doors
Sandra E. Waldron
Olalla, WA
*(Based and developed on an idea by my beloved cousin,
Gracie Nine, now deceased)*

She knew she had been sleeping just seconds ago, but now she was slid-
ing down, down, in a spiral ramp. Opening her eyes, she expected the motion
to stop and find herself back in her bed, but.... no, she was still moving, ever
around and down. Looking around, she saw the dark brick walls with small util-
ity lights, so far apart that the areas she was sliding through were almost totally
obscured. She began to tremble, realizing she was cold and having the sudden
thought, "Just how far down does this thing go?" Just then, the slide began to
shake and she was afraid it would fall under her, but, instead, her speed began
to slow, bringing her to a stop at the bottom. She breathed a sigh of relief until
she looked around. There were six doors, each labeled differently. The names on
the doors were Birth, Love, Hate, Misery, Shame and Death. She sighed heavily.
Now what?

Thinking "Love" would certainly be the one to choose; she stood up and
opened it. Suddenly she found herself flung into a strange new world, donned in
a white wedding dress and staring in a mirror at a stranger, looked Italian, with
a rich complexion and a pleasant face. "Jennifer!" someone called from behind.
"Hurry, dear! You mustn't keep Jim waiting." She swung around and fronted an
attractive but older woman, who slightly resembled the person that had stared
back at her in the mirror.

"Mother?" she said.

"Yes! Hurry!" The older woman grabbed her hand and they went rushing
out to a corridor and into a foyer that opened up into a large, airy church. A
priest in white robes waited for her at the end of the aisle, along with a hand-
some blond man – had to be Jim – and his best man, definitely Italian. Several
young girls, around the age of six, took her train, the music began and an older,
stately man with graying temples took her arm and began leading her down the
aisle. All eyes beheld her. But who was she – really? Jennifer was her name. That
was all she knew.

She felt so strange and out of place, halfway down the aisle she wanted to run. But didn't. Something held her on the path. She stared at her future husband. Handsome! Probably Scandinavian. Such beautiful cool blue eyes. This could not be too bad. Then, with no warning, she was yanked back into the darkness, facing the doors again.

"What?" Totally puzzled, she ran up to the door with the word "Love", but this time it would not open. "Shit!" she exclaimed. "What's going on here?" She stepped back. "Okay...okay...take a deep breath...Jennifer...whatever your name is? And try again." She did. Still the door wouldn't give. She went back and sat down on the end of the ramp for awhile and stared. Okay, she'd try another. She chose "Birth", expecting, if it opened, to be holding a baby in her arms. Instead, she found herself in another dark tunnel, but there was a bright light at the end. She tried to move, but found herself tightly constricted. She realized she wasn't even breathing! Then she was suddenly out in the light and she was being held in the hands of a man. Faces in green masks stared down at her. She was the baby! Well, she thought, maybe this isn't too bad—fresh start, new lease on life. Someone slapped her on her buttocks and she let out a wail, catching a healthy breath of air, but just as she was slipped into her mother's arms, she was whisked back to the dark place, sitting at the bottom of the slide. "Crime-a-nee! What is going on here?" As before with the "Love" door, now the "Birth" door would not open. This was ridiculous. And when was she going to awake from this dream?

Frantically, she surveyed her surroundings – nothing but the darkness and the tiny lights on the walls and the slide, which seemed to go on forever behind her. She sat there for a moment. Should she attempt another door? She had already chosen what she considered the two best of the six. Okay...now...which one? She stood and tentatively reached out her hand, which was shaking now. She decided to go for "Hate". Sure enough, it opened.

She was suddenly in the middle of Nazi Germany in the Second World War; German soldiers were everywhere, grabbing fleeing citizens and forcing them into the back of trucks. One redheaded soldier looked directly at her and yelled, *Frauline!* It was German, but she understood. He pointed to her sleeve. She looked down and realized she wore a band with a six-pointed star. This was definitely not good.

Now she was a Jew! "God help me!" She thought. "Why am I not Italian?" There was a middle-aged woman with stringy salt-and-pepper hair sitting at the back of the truck she was ushered to, "Sarah!" the woman cried out and grabbed her by the arm. The older woman's gray eyes flooded with tears. The soldier yelled at them to shut up and slammed the door and locked it. Sarah looked around and realized the truck was stuffed with many dirty and very sad looking people. "Oh God!" she cried. "Oh God!" The woman was clutching to her and sobbing, mumbling something about Sarah being her little sister.

Sarah kept expecting to be jolted back to the dark place with the slide. But nothing happened. Instead, they rode hour after hour, along a bumpy and winding road. Sometime in the wee hours of the next morning, the truck jolted to a stop. Soon the door opened and the same soldier yelled for them to get out. And he had no patience. He grabbed Sarah by the arm when she didn't move fast enough, bruising her. She barely had time to dust herself off before they were being herded to a long building, surrounded by a barbed wire fence. "Oh my God!" She cried again, recognizing from photos she'd seen in a school book at some time and at someplace – she couldn't remember now – that they were at Belchhammer! A labor camp for Jews.

Once inside, she saw that many were sick. Typhus! "No! God, let me wake up! Please!" The woman that had called her "little sister", still clung to her arm.

The poor woman was exhausted, as now, so was Sarah. They stepped over body after body of sick, beaten people, lying there, hopeless and helpless. The stench was unbearable. Finally, they found a spot where there was enough room on the floor for her and the woman, whom she'd learned was Rachel, to sit down.

Over in a far corner, flies swarmed over piles of feces. Sarah thought surely she would vomit. She turned her face in the other direction and realized that the old white-haired man beside her was dead. She couldn't help it. She screamed!

To her relief, she was at once back in the darkness and sitting on the end of the slide. "Thank you, God!" she cried. "Thank you!" She sat there for a while, trembling, not really sure how long, pondering what door to take next. Surely one would lead her out of this seemingly endless dream. Finally, she stood, took a deep breathe, exhaled and stepped up to "Misery". The door opened very easily.

Someone was standing over her, talking to her, but her head felt like it was going to explode. Pressure! Horrible pressure. The person hovering over her, a handsome man in his early twenties with dark hair, appeared to be shouting. And finally she heard him. "Nancy! Nancy! Can you hear me?"

"Yes…" she said, realizing her voice was weak, shaky. Then it hit her, she couldn't feel anything except for the terrible pain in her head. "What --?"

"Don't try to talk, Nancy," the man said, following her and the gurney into a brightly lit room with huge lamps hanging down from the ceiling. A hospital room! She was quickly hoisted onto an antiseptic-white bed.

"You're at John Sealy," the man said, seeming to understand what she was thinking.

"John Sealy?"

"Yes. In Galveston."

"What happened?"

"You stepped out in front of a car, honey," he answered. "It came around the corner so fast..." then he hushed. He looked as though he was going to cry.

But another man in a white coat came up and stood beside the man that was with her. "Hello, Mr. Adams. I'm Doctor Phillips...the neurologist on duty." He offered his hand and Mr. Adams took it.

"Albert Adams," he said. "It's Albert ."

Doctor Phillips nodded. "Your wife?" he indicated with a nod.

"Yes...my wife. We were just married, not an hour ago. We were so excited...rushing to our car. I yelled for her to wait. I thought I heard a car coming. But she didn't hear me in time. The next thing I knew ..." he started to cry again.

Doctor Phillips took him aside. Nancy couldn't hear what they were saying, but she could tell by her "new" husband's reaction that the doctor wasn't being too encouraging. She lay there and looked around at the bright lights. When was she going to be zapped out of this bad dream and return to the slide? In fact, when was she going to return to her normal life? Whatever that was? She wasn't even sure now.

Someone was beside her, a man in green, sticking a needle in her arm. She could only see it. Not feel it. The only pain was in her head. Then all went black.

When Nancy awoke, she was still on a hospital bed, but in a different room with another bed. Albert was sitting by her and apparently trying very hard not to show his true fears. "Nancy..." he said softly.

"Uh...huh."

"Honey...the news isn't good. The doctor wanted to tell you ...but I thought it best you heard if from me."

She rolled her eyes around to him, looking at him as straight as she could. "Out with it."

"Well... they say your chances of ever walking again are ... are ..." he choked on his words. "I'm sorry," he said. "I thought I could do this..." he jumped up and ran out of the room.

Nancy thought surely she would awaken any moment. But she didn't. A week passed! An entire week! No slide. No dark corridors. No Albert. "God!" she thought. "Please don't keep me in this nightmare! Please!"

But she remained Nancy.

Six grueling months of rehabilitation passed, with the realization that if she didn't return to the slide she would suffer the misery of being trapped in this body-prison for the rest of her life. The days seemed to go on forever. And the nights weren't much better. Would she ever be free of this dream?

A nice young intern by the name of Paul James had taken a special interest in her and, soon as she was able, he took to wheeling her out on the lawn to sit in the sunshine. And they'd have long pleasant talks. He loved Jazz and so did she. He'd bring her CDs to listen to. One day he brought her a Michael Powers CD. She was thrilled, but mad that she couldn't give Paul a hug and told him so. So he gave her a hug.

She still had no memory of who she really was. And her lack of memory was attributed to the accident. And she was no longer upset that Albert never came back. But she was beginning to look forward to Paul's visits – even though she knew it was only a matter of time before she would return to the slide.

But it was taking an awfully long time.

Then one day Paul came in with a long face. He had news that he hated to break to her. It happened that he had finished his internship there and had been offered a job in Dallas. As much as he liked her and would miss her, he couldn't pass up the opportunity.

She did her best to take the news bravely and wished him well, but that night she cried herself to sleep. Yes…this was misery, all right. Maybe she wasn't ever going back to the slide…or to her real life…whatever that was?

But when she opened her eyes the next morning, or so thought that she had, she was back on the slide again, staring at the doors. There was no way she wanted to try "Hate" and "Misery" again. No way! She didn't exactly want to select "Shame" either. How promising could that be? But, there was no way she wanted to pick "Death." She decided on "Shame" and turned the knob, suddenly finding herself flat on her back in a sweat-smelling bed and looking up into the bearded face of a man that reeked of alcohol and stale tobacco—and he was having his way with her. Now she was, indeed, face to face with the meaning of shame. She shoved at him and tried to push him off. It just wasn't happening. "Get off me!" she cried. "Get off!"

"What's ta matta, Peg," the drunk slurred. "Ya like it. Ya know ya do. Least ways that's what you always claim, and I ain't payin' ya sixty dollars fer complainin'."

She turned her head to the side, certain she was going to barf at his hot, stinking breath. But he kept on banging away at her. She finally just shut her eyes tight and held her breath for as long as she could, until she had no choice but to take a gulp of air. She did this—she didn't know how many times—but, finally he was through and rolled off of her, falling instantly into a deep stupor.

"Thank goodness!" She jumped out of the bed and grabbed what she realized had to be her jeans and a red pullover and rushed to the bathroom, not even bothering to grab the red lace bra and panties that lay in the floor just outside the bathroom door. There was a moldy looking shower stall. She thought, "What the hell." And jumped in. There was a half used bar of Ivory in the tray by the cold knob. She turned on the water, let it rush over her body good before lathering up. She scrubbed extra hard between her legs. "Ugh!" she said to herself. "Ugh!"

Soon she was dressed and grabbed a small red purse that had to be hers and ran out the door into the parking lot of a cheap-looking motel. It seemed to be the middle of the night. But where? She walked out into the middle of the lot, finally seeing a broken-down sign that read, Jerry's Sleep-Over. Still, she didn't know what town she was in. What state. She wasn't even sure what country. But the sign was in English. She guessed that was better than nothing. She had a feeling it wasn't England, though.

She started walking in the red pumps. She thought to herself, woman you sure like red...whoever you are. About that time an old Chevy pickup pulled up alongside her and a bald-headed man, wearing a white T-shirt and a gold earring in his left ear, called out to her, "Hey, Peg! Where you going?"

She stopped in her tracks, still full of disgust and furious. "Just leave me alone, Ned." How did she know his name? She had no clue. She just knew. There was something strangely familiar about him, though – like she should know him very well.

"Aw come on, Peggy. Give a man a break, will you? I know I haven't got much, but I can make an honest woman out of you."

She looked down at herself, the way she was dressed. Obviously, she was a whore ... a prostitute. There was no getting around it. And a cheap one at that. Couldn't she at least have been a high-paid one? Then she laughed at the thought. She turned and looked at Ned, still sitting in his truck and waiting for her response.

"Well ...?"

She saw he wasn't going to give in, not by the look on his face. She could only hope she'd be zapped back to the slide before anything else happened. "Okay..." she said. "Okay."

"That's my girl," he said and reached over and opened the passenger door for her.

She ran around the side of the truck and when she sat down, she was back at the slide. "Thank you, God!" she said loudly. "Thank you!"

One door remained – "Death". Did she dare? Or could she, somehow, get back through one of the other doors? But which one? She didn't want to return to any of them except "Love" or "Birth". She jumped up and went up to "Love". With both hands on the knob, she pulled hard. Wouldn't budge. The same went with "Birth". And just for the hell of it, she tried the others – all except "Death". Nope. In a way, she was relieved. She really hadn't wanted to return to the last three, anyway. She went back and sat down. She needed to collect her thoughts.

For some time, she stared and stared at the door to "Death". She knew she had to do something—had to make a decision. And where was all this taking her, anyway? If only she could go back to where it had all begun. If only....But where was that exactly? Now, all she could remember was the darkness and the slide and the tiny lights on the walls. Where – in fact – was she? This thought was stronger with her now than ever before? "Where am I?" She stood once more. She'd been behind all the other doors. There was seemingly no way out … unless "Death" was the way out. But how could "Death" be the way out? The way out of existence maybe. But not the way out of this nightmare. She put her right foot forward, then her left, her right again. Soon, she was there and putting out her shaking hand. She felt the cold metal in her grasp. She turned, clickety-click and pushed.

Nothing but white all around. She couldn't see anything. Not even a hint of a shadow, anywhere. She called out. "Hello!" No one answered. "Hello!" she said again. She turned around. No door. No way back. She made a full three-hundred-and-eighty-degree turn. Still nothing but white. Blinding white. Then suddenly the white was gone and all was darkness. She began to cry. "God! Please don't let this be the end! Please! I don't even know who I am!"

Someone opened the coffin lid. She couldn't move, she couldn't speak, couldn't even breathe. Her eyes were closed, but she could sense people all about. People were crying, some almost uncontrollably. Someone approached the casket. Oh…Alice," a woman's soft voice said. "I am so sorry. I am so sorry I didn't come right when you called. I had no idea you had fallen so hard…. No idea! Please forgive me for not coming right away. Please! I thought you were just doing your usual … complaining. I am so sorry."

Another woman's voice came up right beside the first one. She sounded younger. Perhaps in her twenties. "She can't hear you, Aunt Mildred. She's gone."

"No I'm not! No I'm not!" she said in her mind. "I am very much here. I am very much here!" (Why can't I move?)

Others came to the casket, soon there was a crowd standing around. But it wasn't long and they were gone, maybe to their seats. Music played softly from somewhere, organ music. Someone sang Sweet Hour of Prayer. It would have brought tears to her eyes, if she could have cried. "What is happening? Dear Lord…what is happening?"

The next thing she knew, she was being lowered down into a grave. "No!" she screamed in her head. "No! This can't be it. There has to be a way back. Has to be!"

And suddenly she was sitting at the end of the ramp and staring at the doors. "Thank you, God!" she cried again, wondering how many times she had said that over the past—however long it had been. Was it an eternity? Suddenly the ground was shaking, and with it the slide. Where was there to go? She turned around and stood on the slide and made a desperate attempt to climb up, but it was far too slippery. She slid off onto the ground. Rocks flew and the walls shook. What was she to do? The doors! Would they open now? And, if so, which one did she dare choose?

"Oh dear...oh dear...oh dear." She glanced all around. She could barely stand. The brick walls were coming apart, the little lights falling away. It was growing darker. In desperation, she ran up to the doors. "Which one? Which one? Someone tell me which one?"

Then she suddenly knew which one. And she swung it wide.

Just as they were tossing the last shovel of dirt on her coffin, she felt herself sliding again ...right into the hands of the doctor....

"Good job, Peg," She heard her father say. "She looks just like that old baby photo of my grandmother, Sarah. You know...the one that escaped from Belchhammer."

"Maybe so, Ned, but I want to name her Jennifer after my grandmother. She's the only one in either of our families that had a good life. I'm hoping the name will have good luck for her..."

Baby Jennifer looked up with new eyes at her mother and father. This was going to be a good life. At last, she had chosen the right door at the right time.

R Carlsen
Virginia Beach, VA

stinson beach

it's good to see you again.
my mind floods with memories
of you, she, and myself.
you haven't changed much.
still the little rustic houses
climbing
up the sides
of your hovering mountains.
and small beach houses
on sticks
staring out to sea.
the crashing surf
and old men with fish lines
reaching into the secrets
of your blue waters.
your sand is hot to the feet,
so i must dash around!
nothing new.
7-11 has found you, stinson beach,
i wonder if IBM will too.
i hope not.
i've changed.
i'm a bit more cautious now –
you name it.
i remember like yesterday when
the three of us were together.
on tiny towels necessitating closeness
she and i lay,
tan oiled body to tan oiled body.
she's gone now – but i've returned.
next time i'll bring a close friend of mine.
i know that you would like her.
i'll try to bring her soon.
i've missed you.

R. Carlsen

carmel

it's always nice
to travel your streets
and alleyways,
and search out
the secrets and pleasures
of your mystic domain.
with your quaint shops
sometimes hidden behind
those paying front footage,
your white-sand beaches
with grains that speak to the feet,
and driftwood that
feeds the imagination.
you are tranquility
to a cluttered mind,
and an empty wallet
to the unwary tourist.
you also hold memories
for me
of love on the beach
at nightfall.
i've come to you before
just to have your name
on the box of a necklace
for someone special.
you have a strong hold
on me,
so i'll be back soon.

Paris et ses Ruines

By: Michelle Honora Wagreich
Woodbridge, VA

"As I was saying William," I said trying to draw his attention back to me. For some reason, he was always distracted by something on our Sunday walks. "Greater faith in human reason and empirical observation as a source of truth and as a means to improve the physical and social environment can only be bolstered by scientific discoveries despite crackpot theoretical morons like Galileo who believe otherwise. Now take that idiot Spinoza who called for political and intellectual freedom and developed a systematic rationalistic philosophy. I tell you William, that is just the most audacious front to human reason in history. What made that imbecile think by developing, what he called Ethics, it would solve whatever problems he assumed, like the narrow-minded bigot he is, there were with philosophy?"

"He didn't say there was something wrong with human philosophy, William returned. "He and someone like Voltaire for instance."

"Voltaire!" I exclaimed wondering how William had the nerve to mention such a man to me. "You mean that demented lunatic who wrote diaries and novels about exotic travels to illustrate the so-called 'intellectual trend towards secular ethics and relativism'? How the moron even knows what 'intellectual' means is beyond my comprehension. While we are on this topic though, let us not exclude that other half-wit Descartes who used a rational approach modeled on geometry (Geometry of all things!) to discover what he called 'self evident truths' as a foundation for knowledge. Really, that just makes me sick to my stomach. Next thing you know, people will go around using math to walk across the street. Utterly shameful and ridiculous!" I shook my head and paused upon the sidewalk. There were many out today as several horse and carriages were passing here and there on the street, but I doubted they were really going anywhere specific.

"But what's wrong with trying to rationalize truth by using geometry?" William demanded.

"First of all, self-truth can not be rationalized since thoughts can not be placed into numbers. I am not talking to you in mathematics am I? No, and therefore, if my thoughts are in words, what makes anyone think they can rationalize what I believe to be as truth in numbers? Do you really expect me to describe your coat by saying 'ah what a fine three times seven'?"

"That isn't what he's saying at all. You're just trying to ridicule his ideas because they don't fit your own," William scolded. He looked about ready to snatch away my cookie.

I sighed and straightened up my top hat. "Truth, William, is whatever I want it to be and when I say 'I' I am not implying myself in the lateral sense, I am merely using it as a metaphor to mean the human who stands up to speak for it. Truth does not necessarily mean reality since there are many truths of this world, since there are many different people in this world who look at truth differently. Truth actually has no value. It is more like a liquid with no solid shape. It molds to fit a particular society. And since it has no actual value it, therefore, cannot be rationalized by mathematics."

"Bosh! You can't expect me to believe truth's valueless." William waved a hand at me in protest. "Besides, there are some truths that can't be 'molded into society' as you put it." When he saw me arch an eyebrow, he continued. "Take the sky for example. It's blue and no matter what society you grow up in, the sky will always be blue."

I wanted to laugh but refrained myself. "But William," I countered, "the sky is not always blue because it reflects many colors and the color it reflects the strongest at that particular hour is the color you see. Look up at the sky right now and see for yourself it is a hazy gray, like when it snows, though it will do no such a thing this time of year." Just ahead of us, on the sidewalk, was a gentleman standing in the middle of another gentleman and a woman. The woman was on the side that faced the street and I watched as two soldiers in full uniform passed by and smiled at her. They were riding horses and both carried a small flag.

"All right then," William said refusing to admit defeat. "Take that lamppost over there. No matter who you are, you can't argue it isn't a lamppost." It was clear he did not let the riders' presence interfere with his conversation.

I looked at William confused, tightened the grip on my walking cane and asked, "Who said I could not argue that it is not a lamppost. For that matter, if I wanted to argue it was not, who in the world could stop me?"

William looked at me with a skeptical glance. "No one," he said stiffly, "they wouldn't have to because people would just take you for insane and walk away."

There it was and this time I had to laugh. I watched the lad's face turn red and knew I had to explain something. "Insane is a rather strong word and I would never consider myself in league with demented people like Newton. I mean really, how could such a man get worldly praise for just emphasizing an induction form of experimental observations? The nerve of him to claim he discovered something, which he named gravity! Ha! More likely, the bong on the head affected what little brain he had, if he had one at all. That, however, is getting off the subject. You claim I would be insane if I argued the fact that the lamppost is not a lamppost. Well, the same thing happens in court everyday and no one calls lawyers insane, so what difference are they to me?"

"Lawyers don't argue that lampposts aren't lampposts." William returned haughtily.

I sighed wondering if William, though I know he heard me, listened to a word I said. "Did I not just get finished saying that truth is whatever I want it to be? That is what I mean, William. In court, there are two truths, but both are whatever the person defending it wants it to be. The first truth is 'actual' truth, and the second is 'provable' truth. Not necessarily are they the same since one may have a hard time proving what actual truth is without proof. That is what is wrong with the justice system since truth is no longer truth unless it is provable fact. No one can just accept truth anymore unless it is fact based like the lamppost. If I argued it was not, of course, no one would believe me, but if I brought out 'unquestionable proof' to prove my case, everyone would believe me. Why should truth need to be proven? That is because no one believes in truth anymore since no one knows what it is anymore —like if I said the truth was that lamppost was not a lamppost."

"But of course it's a lamppost. Everyone knows that's what it is! That's absolutely ridiculous!" William shook his head.

"I see. You clearly are doing exactly what I am trying to make you not do. Think of the lamppost in metaphorical terms. I am saying a statement 'the lamppost is not a lamppost' and what are you doing? You are saying, 'Yes it is.' Why should my truth be different that yours simply because yours is face value? Since when does truth need a 'face value'?" I sighed, rather sadly, as I looked at the lamppost. "Truth has become lost, twisted, or warped with no value any-more because society as a whole has lost its reason for believing in truth. No one protects the truth anymore much like justice and laws basically protect the criminals and not good citizens. What good is having a law since it does not really serve any purpose?"

"How can you say there's no reason to have laws? If there weren't laws or law makers…"

"Then," I said, interrupting William before he had the chance to embarrass himself, "totally imbecilic crooks would not be able to fool gullible people by robbing them of their money by making false promises which anyone with half-a-brain would know they cannot keep."

"You can't make such a rational comment about certain people in society by saying they all have degrading characteristics of human nature like racism, prejudice, narrow-mindedness, intolerance, dogmatism, fanaticism, sexism, bigotry, and injustice," William snapped.

I reached up and twisted the tip end of my mustache, yawned and shook my head at William. "One word would have sufficed and had the same effect as all the others. It is as if you would have said something to the effect of, 'Professor, you are much older than I and therefore think you know more about the ways of the world than I do, but in all truthful, frank, straightforward honesty, you do not.'"

"That," William responded trying to control his anger, "is a true statement."

"I am saying that there is no reason to waste words when the shortest possible explanation gets the same result."

"Sometimes your explanations," William returned, his voice clearly teetering on the edge of anger, "don't get the same results because you want me to think like you, but there's no fact behind it. They're your opinions, and you won't even admit that since you're self-deluded in thinking that your comments are the only real truth in this world."

"I do not think that since I prefer you to be an independent thinker. I am merely pointing out long explanations of the same truth are wasteful. Really William! There is a definite strong difference between long explanations and the short cut. The long is a line not a circle as your friend Descartes would say. What is that famous line, ah yes, 'I think therefore I am'. He would have done himself more justice had he said, 'I think, therefore I am a moron'. But that is getting off the subject. The short has no chance of one losing attention where as the attention of audiences' loses interest in the long." I watched his eyes glitter in anger, and wished he was not so sensitive.

Hoping to calm him down I shrugged. "Maybe I am wrong…in a way." I saw the anger subside slightly and then said, "Perhaps the real problem with society is not the explanation of truth, but those who claim they know the real truth. Those crackpot philosophers like Descartes, but not just him; I mean all of them. Why does society really need them? All they do is sit around and think. Actually, if that were all they did, then they would not be such a menace. They chose to write what they think into books and bookshops stack the books on their shelves and people like you buy the books and start thinking the exact same thing. That, I think, breeds a heck of a lot more chaos than order in people's minds."

The anger was back in his eyes. "Not everything in chaos is chaotic. Something must be chaotic for order to be established. For example, war is not just bloodshed. When there's war, a lot of new inventions evolve which makes the war end sooner and without the war they never would have been invented,"

He snapped angrily. William did not hesitate to make me know his temperature was boiling.

I, on the other hand, remained calm since I never allow my conversations to get emotional or personal. "Yet if there was no war, the inventions would not have been needed to be invented in the first place." I watched William and leaned a bit harder on my walking stick. "What is this? The 'Enlightenment Period'? What have we to be 'enlightened' about anyway? Perhaps people like that blockhead mule Rousseau will teach us what we are to be 'enlightened' about. Rousseau's radical concepts of 'social contract and of inherent goodness of common man gave impetus to antimonarchical republicanism' is just long complicated blabber that, since no one understands, everyone thinks is brilliant. Perhaps he, like that flake Hume who radically reduced the role of reason in philosophy, think that the rest of us are idiots trapped in some kind of darkness and feel the need to 'enlighten' us. What makes them think that writing their idiotic thoughts down on paper would 'enlighten' anyone about anything? For that matter, who says that we, the people of France of the 19th century, need to be 'enlightened' in the first place?

"Nothing they have said can change the way people think unless they are gullible and therefore a useless piece of space. Our country, William, has had its Revolutions and invasions. We have survived the aristocratic beheadings of Robespierre, which served no purpose anyway. I mean, yes, the aristocrats made the poor people unhappy and 'had it coming' but look at what happened. Everyone was starting to be beheaded because there was no more upper crust to behead which caused us to end up with an upstart on the throne that is not even French! After knowing all this and coming to your own truth about the whole thing, you could not possibly tell me philosophers or government officials know real truth and we, the commoner whose job it is to listen to those brainless men, know nothing of real truth. How can you stand there and say they, rather than I, deserve respect and admiration?"

"You? Respect and admiration!" William shouted. A few on the street turned and looked at us, but I ignored them. William, however, took his voice down a notch. "I believe they all have a purpose in life and are meant to do the job for which they do like Plato and Aristotle. They have found peace or truth in their life and want to share it with the rest of us. They cannot be completely truthful with themselves, if their life means nothing, and it won't have value unless they have achieved something. In order to achieve a life of strong truthful meaning and value, one must have conquered someone or something. If everything in a person's life was free and easy to get, there is something very wrong with that person's life."

"So," I said, after a long moment of consideration, "the only way I could feel I have accomplished something in my life is by beating you up?" Perhaps that was a bit crude, but I wanted William to see that what he was trying to convince me of was just as crude.

"I didn't say that," William snapped, his eyes now completely glaring with anger. "All I'm saying is that life can't exist without obstacles. The way a person handles them makes him stronger and his life more valuable."

"And I agree," I responded with as much composure as I could muster. I knew my calmness was what drove William angry, but I just could not help myself. "However, you can not tell me that an act of violence, in the end, is an act of charity. If you were suggesting that is what you mean, you are no better than that bumbling nitwit Locke. Look William, we all want a fulfilling life that has meaning and order rather than chaos. We are all looking for a truth, our reason and philosophy, but we will never find it with all these idiots running around and confusing the younger generation. Society has a way of breeding conformity and conformity is the only order to life. That much you have to admit."

William was so angry he narrowed his eyes at me and clutched the walking stick until his knuckles were white. "I don't have to agree with a thing you say." He snapped. "If everyone was a conformist, we'd never have leaders in government or anything. We need radicals who punch holes in the system in-order for people to live a better meaningful life."

"Look at us," I shook my head with authority as I waved my hand at the people around us. "All the gentlefolk are conformist and there is nothing wrong with it. All the ladies have bonnets and long gowns and the men are wearing overcoats with a walking cane and top hat. Why look at you! Despite the fact that you deny 'molding into society and conforming' by wearing that drab red coat, you still wear the conventional top hat. Your own fears of radicalism will not let you be radical so instinctively you take your top hat and walking cane. People pass and marvel at your coat, but they also know you are a gentleman by your hat and cane. A gradual change, William, is not radical."

"Then I won't wear it!" William snapped in as much rage as I had ever seen and reached up and took it off his head. Then, much to my surprise, he threw it into the street.

I looked at him sadly. "Loitering? Must I venture into that limb of conversation?"

William narrowed his eyes at me and it was clear he would punch me. He refrained, however, and just made fists at his sides. "Your narrow-minded aristocratic ideals make me sick." He then turned his back on me and marched down the street. I watched him disappear around the corner as I picked up his hat and dusted it off. I then smiled, knowing we would have the exact conversation when we met again next Sunday.

Diana Festa
New York

Needy

Unprovoked, questions come up, will I, will you?
Tell me, will you take the walk with me
across the wood, hold my hand
not to stumble on dead trunks,
will you push the branches to the side
for me to pass?

In Central Park so innocuous, my foot bled,
the shoe a vise, I did not tell you,
my offering.

I want you to know, at Arles by the haystacks,
I felt Van Gogh's desperate loneliness,
the unmerciful sky. The depth of his yellows,
the startled eyes in sunflowers nudged
my unresisting sinews, heat burned my scalp.
And did you see the window in Piazza Farnese looking
down, it condemned me to microscopic indignities,
to remove the smudge from my white shirt.

I expected you to know the things
I may have imagined, I
peddler of recognition in the art of dissembling
insufficiency.

You gave me a lot, I am grateful,
I wanted more,
how to banish the image of a shut door
in the juxtaposition of fear and desire.

Diana Festa

Les yeux du pere disaient: "Que c'est beau! que c'est beau!
On dirait que tout l'or du pauvre monde est venu se porter
sur ces murs."
*Baudelaire: **Les Yeux des Pauvres.***

Carnival

The painted faces of Venetian masks centuries ago,
still now,
tragic, comic, frightful, gay,
and costumes in rainbow tints
for revelries, dreams on marble steps,
they fill shops along watery calli reflecting
shadows of scattered days.

A face looks from the other side
at the merrymaking, wedges an intruding presence
on the dance floor, the sipping of champagne
through the night.

Life hangs on threads I twist
round my wrists. Seen from the fringe, my face pressed
against the pane outside
the hall where walls tremble,
mirrors deform the circle of dancers.

I walk heavy steps to the river's edge,
the wind whistles, or maybe
strains of songs from the party linger to dawn.
Years waver undecided if to loosen
the grip on time past,
let go
cotillions, masks pitted against censure,
that face outside the palace.

I think of Fall and Winter, of waters
graying in the cold, and reach for the mask hanging
on my wall, the careful golds on fragile features,
and the reds,
bright on eyes where pain has dried.

At the Stronghold for Renegade Bodies

By Josh Morsell
Mendocino, CA

Ridge Rodson spread his clawed wings and glanced to the rafters. Shadows of rats there. Usually they scuttled fast, but tonight they were still, huddled and nibbling conspiratorially. Rodson knew these might be no normal rats; in a house such as this nothing could be assumed normal.

His own engineering had been for a peculiar vanity; old Dr. Thaddeus Pekaw wanted to show he could surpass the generative surgeons and then infect their thinking with his own. Deliberately, Pekaw had planted in Rodson's back not just wings, considered beautiful even if unnatural; but wings with clawed hands at their ends, monstrous and more useful.

Rodson was a captive to Pekaw, held for years while the doctor monitored his patient's growth and prepared for the day of unveiling. Within the garden walls of the Stronghold for Renegade Bodies, Pekaw's lair and pioneering laboratory, Rodson had read the old man's books. He understood Pekaw's principles of Unregenerate Masculinity, Desired Female Sexuality, So-Called Perversion of Race Characteristics, and the Undesirability of the Manifest. Rodson remembered the world outside, the stalkings in a jungle of artifice that comprised 22nd Century Polyland. Fabulous as that Oz might be, "No place like home" meant for so many normal people a pull to stable (i.e. imaginary) Edens: summer popsicles, predictable sexualities, the old family house unravaged by time. Soon, if Pekaw could help it, people would yearn too for stable morphology.

If Pekaw could help it and if Rodson could help it. Rodson would soon be going on tour, and Pekaw had implanted a brain chip to inflict pain if he didn't cooperate. But Pekaw hoped, and Rodson knew, that chip wouldn't likely be necessary. Rodson was intelligent enough to have recognized the subtle reason to Pekaw's crimes against him. He respected the messianic urgency of Pekaw's project and as such submitted enthusiastically to the man's daring.

"What, Ridge?" Pekaw snapped up from his scribblings irritably, the phonograph blasting Paganini's Caprice no. 24.

Rodson had entered the room behind Pekaw, who sat in an armchair the stuffed feet of which had been harvested from an earlier experiment in generative surgery. Rodson thoughtfully scratched a talon along the webbing of one wing. "Dr. Pekaw, I've been watching the frogs and I thought they could use wings like flying fish. The wings would have to be streamlined under water, of course."

"That is so far down my priority list." Pekaw resumed scribbling. Rodson shuffled out. He didn't mind. He just thought the idea might be useful to Pekaw. He didn't want to disturb him. He did often wonder, though, if Pekaw was watching while Rodson did his own experiments. He hoped so. He wanted the old man's approval. He imagined Pekaw smiling benevolently at Rodson's youthful competence.

Rodson nearly tripped over the dog-sized mouse that scuttled in front of him, prehensile monkey's tail creepy as always to Rodson. A flight of fancy, he thought. He was independent enough to critique the old man, who had given the mouse a cat's brain, some vicious joke. The previously attempted mouse had a snake's brain, but it didn't grow properly and it died.

It was only then that Rodson noticed, a crack ajar, a door in a motley wall where he never knew a door to be: a hidden door that had not been properly shut!

He could not resist; at a high point in the fury erupting from the phonograph, Rodson parted the portal (just a little squeal of the hinge!) and, lighting his tiny blue keychain light, descended the stairs he found, pulling the door shut completely behind him.

As Rodson crept downward, his wings scraped the low ceiling and the spiderwebs that clung there. Rodson shuddered, reflexively flicking the sticky webs from his skin. Then, "Ouch!"

Startled by a spider bite, Rodson leapt around to ascend the stairs; but through his panic he heard, from the dark below-behind him, "Wait."

Now Rodson swung back toward the spiders. Who was down there? "Hello?"

A man's voice. "Though you may not know it, I have the sight of a deep sea fish, able to detect light under miles of water. I'd appreciate it if you'd turn off that blue light, it burns my eyes."

"Uh. Do you live here?" Rodson couldn't see the man.

"I can't leave here. Except on nights when there's a new moon."

"I can't see you."

The man chuckled. "We could be Beauty and the Beast."

"Why are your eyes like that?"

"I wanted to be able to crawl around in the bushes at night. Seriously. I like to watch animals that come out. For several years, really, I spent most of my waking hours creeping around in the dark watching stuff. I'm not much for socializing."

Rodson wondered why the man had stopped him if the latter was true. The man continued, "Thaddeus did this for me. We didn't realize how sensitive

I would be. Could you go up and get me food? They never turn the lights off, I can't go up there. I'm a vegetarian, so like bread and hummus or something?"

"Does Dr. Pekaw know you're down here?"

Dr. Pekaw had wired a microphone and was listening.

Pekaw's first hallucinations came when he was twenty-seven. A voice that startled him by shouting his name. Then he noticed that the father of a woman with whom he was involved, an exceptionally jealous and menacing man, began to flash before his eyes whenever he saw someone of roughly the same body type. Then he no longer needed a human signifier: round a corner and he'd jump to see the man, who would vanish into the empty street. Pekaw also had striking dreams. He was staying up late, sleeping until noon. Some alchemy of sunlight brought to his morning slumber vivid repetitions of powerful monstrous figures with claws, wings, tails and human faces, and always Pekaw felt the same emotions: excitement, intimacy, danger, wariness. He felt those again when he started seeing the beasts in waking hours, replacing the father: demons in the city, in the woods, in the air. He instinctively thought these visions a great breakthrough, but he feared that unanchored to reality they would overwhelm him. He decided to make them real, and kidnapped the luscious boy Ridge Rodson.

Fisheye was telling Rodson about the radio shows he listened to. "I put on my headphones and listen while I walk around and look for animals. Watch the birds hop in the bushes while I listen to the news. Those bastards in the White House! It really is criminal what they're doing. But it's what they've always done, I guess, under one name or another."

Rodson felt himself strangely jealous at the existence of this man, and wondered at Pekaw's motivations with him. He was starting to feel woozy, he guessed from the spider bite. Memories of his operation surfaced, and Pekaw's passionate words: "...make dreams real... harness the power of phantasms... transcend your subjectivity..." At the time Pekaw's notions and the changes wrought had terrified Rodson, but then they brought unexpected developments in him. They had given him a means to gain advantage in the world, and they had thereby given him purpose. Rodson carried a faith that was impregnable, and made him at once sure and flexible, expressed, as Pekaw had taught him, by Yeats:

> Do not wait to strike
> Till the iron is hot;
> But make it hot
> By striking.

And yet... he would have to strike at the proper time. Rodson, the future freak messiah, had long been waiting, long preparing.

Fisheye was talking now about his sailing trip to Mexico before he had the transplant. Rodson was starting to wheeze. He interrupted Fisheye. "I was bit by a spider."

"Is it serious?"

He'd been waiting to find out. "I don't know."

"Do you want to sit down?"

"I'm okay. So, how did you meet Dr. Pekaw?"

"Thaddeus and I were friends back in Aspen."

Rodson had heard older people explain themselves this way before. He didn't know what had happened in Aspen once upon a time, but to people who had been there it counted for a lot.

"I have to sit down." Rodson was dizzy and his head hurt; his breath was near gasping.

"We better get you checked out. Can you make it up the stairs to Thaddeus?"

But Rodson was already lying on the cold and dirty basement floor. Fisheye moved toward him. "I'm going to carry you." He'd just have to close his eyes.

But then Pekaw was at the top of the stairs. "Ridge?"

Fisheye called, "I'm glad you're here, Thad! Ridge's been bit by a spider and he's not doing well."

"Oh? Ridge, what's going on?"

Rodson interpreted Pekaw's tone as one of clinical interest, and this pained him; but he hadn't the will, or maybe the ability, to respond. He felt none of the panic he'd have expected from suffocation. Instead, syrupy nausea, an aching, swollen bite, a pounding head, and a little sadness. He wheezed pathetically, no fierce effort for oxygen.

Pekaw grew alarmed and rushed down the stairs into the dark. "Jiles, help me get him to the light."

Rodson dimly felt himself hoisted off the ground, carried up the stairs. He would later describe his febrile reaction to the venom:

"A slave's triumph I felt while the bite turned blue and pain burned its aurora through my wing. I knew it meant the failure of what I had worked for; but it also meant freedom from what I did not want. A slave who would not conspicuously defy, and so instead pretends he did not summon his attackers."

Thud. In agitated distraction, Pekaw had dropped Rodson's upper half on the kitchen's cold linoleum. Fisheye winced, and gingerly set down the boy's legs. Then he retreated into the dark stairwell, lids slitted against what was to him blazingly bright light. Pekaw felt Rodson's neck: just the hint of a pulse, and then it faded and was gone. Pekaw frantically attempted CPR, to no avail.

"Damn that spider! Jiles, he's dead."

From behind the door, Fisheye said, "Thad, I'm sorry."

In a strange way, Pekaw felt relieved and emboldened. Years of work were gone, his plans dashed. Now Thaddeus Pekaw was free to do anything.

Except Ridge Rodson wasn't really dead.

What Fate Decrees

By Sheila M. Roberson
Westminster, MD

From the deck of the *Talisman*, Adam Mason, a shipwrecked sailor from the *Sussex*, listened with horror at the harsh rasping sound echoing ominously throughout the imperiled ship as she grated back and forth across the reef. Surmising that he had brought the curse aboard with him, Adam was unable to prevent thoughts flooding into his mind about events that led up to this second calamity.

After a tumultuous journey around Cape Horn, the *Sussex* sailed into the Pacific Ocean. It was 1823 and more ships were venturing into the South Seas with many casting anchor at New Zealand's Bay of Islands. The Sussex, however, risked the treacherous sandbar that stretched across the entrance to Hokianga harbor on the opposite coast and anchored at the mouth of the harbor's inlet.

No sooner, though, had the sailors furled the ship's sails than the local Maori chief and some of his tribesmen came aboard to trade shrunken heads for muskets and powder, and while they sojourned on the ship the chief decided to give the crew a friendly warning about the danger ashore. After adjusting his knee-length flax skirt about his tattooed brown torso, he squatted on the deck beside his fellow tribesmen and began telling the off-duty sailors the legend of the harbor's sacred rock. In reverential tones, he explained that the god of wind and waves resided within the rock and held sway over the surrounding waters.

The chief paused to secure the three red feathers in his topknot of black hair and then leaned forward on his haunches and warned that any person foolish enough to offend this vengeful deity risked certain death. Next, he delivered his coup de grace and in a hoarse whisper related that over the years many tribesmen had drowned when the angry god capsized their canoes. Some of the seamen listened with skepticism, others were curious, but a few had a mariner's instinctive sense of danger and listened with foreboding.

When swabbing the deck the following morning, Adam gazed shoreward in search of the mysterious bastion. "First chance I get I'm gonna visit that rock," he told Tim, a fellow seaman.

"Well, don't count on me. I ain't goin' near the cursed thing!"

"You scared?" asked Adam, brushing aside the mat of blond hair that fell across his freckled forehead.

Tim's denial, although vociferous, was sheepish, "I ain't scared but I ain't goin'!"

That afternoon, the first mate sent Adam, Tim, and three fellow seamen ashore for a supply of fresh water, but before returning to the ship with the loaded barrels Adam decided to put the tale of the rock-dwelling god to the test. He persuaded two Maoris to lead him to the god's sanctuary, and unaware of his intentions they agreed. With the unwilling Tim, whom he had coerced into accompanying him, Adam followed his Maori guides to the site.

Ignorant of the cultural heritage the rock held for the local tribesmen and careless of their beliefs, Adam stooped before the tapued (forbidden) pillar and, smirking, muttered, "I'll show that god what's what!" Then, to the horror of the watching Maoris, he struck the rock forcefully with a large stone, knelt and put his ear to the revered sanctuary and listened for any sounds of activity within. Hearing nothing, he began beating the rock again, and regardless of the Maoris' terrified remonstrations he continued striking it until deciding that perhaps the legend lacked substance.

A few days later, the Sussex weighed anchor to depart Hokianga, but before leaving his cabin to return to the deck Captain Knox gazed with fascination at the shrunken head resting on his teak table. Although the macabre object stared back at him from haunted eyes he felt no fear, for Knox knew that the ghoulish relic would sell for a sizeable sum in Sydney. Satisfied that he had made a good trade, he patted the object atop its head of black hair and departed the cabin.

A light breeze was blowing and Knox relied on this to carry the ship out beyond the treacherous sand bar, but when the Sussex reached the formidable barrier, the wind failed her. Earlier, a belligerent south-west wind had stirred up unusually high surf, and the returning tide brought pounding waves that raced shoreward and beat relentlessly against the hull of the beleaguered ship. Maliciously they spun her around and mercilessly they drove her shoreward. She struck the rocks stern first with all sails set and in no more than two hours the Sussex was reduced to wreckage. Although there was no loss of life, all provisions, cargo, and personal possessions were lost.

Local tribesmen rescued the bereft seamen and gave them shelter overnight. The next day the Maoris provided guides to lead the stranded seamen overland to the Bay of Islands, and after five days struggling through bush the bedraggled group reached Kororareka,* where the whalers *New England Legend* and *The Pride of Massachusetts* were anchored. The two ships accommodated as many of the shipwrecked sailors as possible, and three months later Adam, Tim, and the remaining seamen were given passage on the *Talisman*. They were to work their way back to Sydney.

As the *Talisman* prepared to depart Kororareka, the moon was still visible, and when eight bells sounded the morning watch relieved the mid-watch. The crews exchanged greetings in passing, and the morning watch proceeded to the starboard bow while the departing watch went below. In his cabin, Captain Maxwell stood studying his charts, but the overhead whale-oil lamp swung back and forth, alternately removing and returning its light to the table. Exasperated, he swept the charts aside and after pushing his arms into the sleeves of an all-weather coat, he strode out of his cabin and onto the deck.

A belligerent easterly wind blew across Kororareka Bay, and although riding at anchor the *Talisman* was lifted back and forth by the choppy swells. Catching sight of a small knot of deckhands shivering in the early morning chill, the boatswain diverted his attention from the seamen up in the rigging readying sail for departure and yelled, "Look lively, you landlubbers!"

From the quarterdeck, the captain watched the few passengers boarding his ship, one of whom was John Kaine, a departing missionary. Then, after a flurry of last-minute activities, the mate yelled to sailors at the windlass, "Break out anchor, lads!"

The ship worked her way from Kororareka, but with the wind dead on the land she labored to maintain her course. Reaching up and pulling at Adam's arm, the pessimistic Tim pointed upward, "Y'know the old sayin', Adam, a red sky in the mornin's a sailor's warnin'." Adam, however, was in no mood to talk and moved away.

With blustering clouds chasing one another across the grey sky, the weather worsened, and the snapping sound of wind tearing into canvas sent sailors up the ratlines to shorten sail, but their efforts to stay the ship's course failed, and the *Talisman* was beaten towards the rocky shoreline. With worry lines creasing his brow, Captain Maxwell decided to try a series of tacks and yelled to the helmsman, "Bring her hard alee!" When the helmsman's efforts failed to turn the ship about, Maxwell, hoping the *Talisman* could ride out the gale, yelled to the mate, "Drop anchor!"

"Perhaps she'll sit safely in this spot," murmured Tim, listening apprehensively to the rattle of chains as the anchor cable slid down the ship's side and crashed into the angry, dark water.

Long years at sea had given Maxwell a keen sense of danger and beckoning to Adam he yelled, "You there, over here! Get to the side, lad, and swing the lead!"

Instantly aware of what was expected of him, Adam crossed the deck to the gunwales and dropped over the ship's side onto a small chained platform below. Then, with the lead line coiled at his feet he whirled the twenty fathoms of line seaward, while loosely holding the bight of line in his left hand to feel the marks as the line plummeted to the bottom. With rain running off his cap in rivulets, the captain, nervously clenching and unclenching his hands, stood waiting for the reading.

"By the mark three fathoms!" yelled Adam.

"What's that you say?" roared the captain, hoping that Adam had erred. "No more than three fathoms below us? Heave-ho the line again, lad, and get it right this time!"

Soon Adam was back. "Like I said, sir, she's sitting in three fathoms." Then, with a nervous spate of words, he delivered the rest of his findings, "And she's lying on the edge of a reef!"

Maxwell's face was the color of the whitecaps below. Too shocked to voice his usual curses, he spluttered, "Merciful Mary, Mother of God, how can this be!"

"Them black clouds, they been movin' from east to west all mornin' instead of from west to east," muttered Tim to a nearby seaman. Then, running his hands through his shock of red hair, he added, "Mark my words, 'tis a bad omen!"

As the day progressed, the wind grew more violent with heavy swells rolling in and striking the beleaguered *Talisman* as they raced landward. Later, torrential rains fell, and what had been heavy swells earlier now became towering waves that roared up to the bulwarks and flooded onto the ship's deck. Then, at the turn of the tide the captain's worst fears were realized, for the *Talisman* struck the reef. However, in spite of her perilous position, Maxwell was confident that once the tide was out his ship would remain firm on the reef and, thus, was in no immediate danger of breaking up.

Soon, night captured what little light the forlorn grey day had provided, and although it hid the visual reality of the dangerous situation, it provided no relief. In the pitch darkness below decks passengers' moments of fitful dozing were interrupted by the jarring impact of wind and wave on the ship's hull.

As Adam stood watch, the *Talisman*'s plight forced him to face reality. Believing that he was responsible for the wreck of the *Sussex* and blaming himself for the *Talisman*'s peril, he focused on his actions on the fateful day in Hokianga when, with carefree indifference, he had unleashed the vengeance of the Maoris' god of wind and waves by dishonoring the deity and striking the sanctuary wherein he dwelt.

In an attempt to rid his mind of these incriminating thoughts, Adam began to consider his future and the more he concentrated on this strange subject, the more he realized that his life lacked purpose. Discomforted by this evaluation he dismissed these thoughts too. In this rare introspective mood, Adam told himself that he should have been more respectful to his Maori guides and more tolerant of their beliefs. "Respectful? Tolerant?" He raised his eyebrows at both the words and the alien thoughts they engendered, muttering, "Aw, I'm a sailor, not a saint."

Once more the bells sounded and Adam's watch ended, but as he approached the hatchway a crashing impact on the ship's timbers flooded his mind with fear and he went below convinced that the Maoris' god had marked him for death.

When daylight broke over the grey sea, Kaine, the missionary, concerned about the safety of the passengers approached the captain and with the wind raging around him expressed his concerns to Maxwell, "We must get the passengers and as many of the crew as possible to the safety of that island off in the distance."

Indicating sailors with a sweep of his hand, Maxwell responded with sarcastic impatience, "You tend to your flock, parson, and I'll tend to mine! And as for taking the passengers to that island, what do you know about the natives on those shores? They're cannibals, I tell you—all cannibals!"

"That may be so, Captain Maxwell, but misguided as these Maoris may be they're God's children, nonetheless." Then with the confidence born of faith, Kaine added, "And with God's help we'll reach that island safely and when onshore God will continue to protect and guide us."

Placing the glass to his eye, Maxwell focused it toward the distant fog-covered shore. "Well, be aware that you go at your own risk!" Then he emitted a shrill whistle, and within moments the coxswain was at his side. "See to it that one of the boats is lowered," he ordered.

Despite the ambiguity of what might await them ashore, the passengers were anxious to leave the *Talisman*. "Stand by to lower," commanded the coxswain once the passengers were seated in the quarter-boat. The oarsmen found their positions on the thwarts and sailors lowered the boat to the dark, threatening sea.

In an effort to bolster the spirits of those in the quarter-boat, Kaine shouted words of encouragement to them. "Be of good faith, for all things work together for good for those that love the Lord."

Regardless of the storm, the wind carried Kaine's words to sailors on the *Talisman*'s deck. They meant nothing to Adam, for the ear-splitting sound of wind and waves brought another powerful surge of fear to his mind, convincing him that death was now ready to claim him. Then a light across the troubled water caught his eye.

Thinking the light might be that of a ship ghosting through the gloom, Adam searched for the vessel's outline, but as he watched, the light seemed to grow brighter and he saw what appeared to be a luminous figure just above the raging water. Convinced that his imagination was playing tricks on him, Adam rubbed his eyes and looked again. Then he stared in disbelief as the figure emitting the radiant light reached out to him.

Fear, rapier-sharp, penetrated Adam's body and his knees buckled beneath him, but just as his trembling hands grasped the ship's railing for support he heard a voice resonating within him--a soundless voice that activated every nerve in his body, "Fear not and know that I am God!"

The soul-searing words took command of Adam's heart and mind and instantly fear fell away from him. It was replaced by a powerful sense of well-being and purpose. He searched across the water again, but the figure was gone.

As Adam turned to cross the deck, Tim approached him. With his words etched with fear, Tim announced, "We've gotta get off this ship right now, Adam, before the Maoris' god gets us!"

Adam placed one hand on his friend's shoulder reassuringly and with the other he pointed heavenward, telling Tim, "There's only one god, Tim. The Maoris don't know it yet but one day soon they will." As Adam crossed the deck to go below, his purpose in life was established. He would join the few missionaries at the Bay of Islands and help spread the Lord's word in this far-flung land.

The *Talisman* broke up one week after striking the reef, but before the ship wrecked, Maoris transported the captain and his crew to the nearby island where, despite Maxwell's fears for the safety of his sailors, they were given food and shelter. Later, the Maoris transported the survivors to Kororareka, but at Adam's request they took him across the Bay of Islands to the mission settlement.

*Kororareka is present-day Russell at the Bay of Islands, New Zealand

Tremors

by Tessa Nelson-Humphries
Las Cruces NM

"To exorcise the demons of memory
it is sometimes necessary to tell them as a story."
Isabel Allende

Narcisa Pacheco still felt as shaky as the tectonic plates forever shifting under Chile's narrow shape. Of many men whose lives she'd erupted through, Felipe Justo, orthopedic surgeon, had caused her still-rolling tremors before suddenly dumping her for a wealthy older widow. As if that weren't seismic enough, the top law firm she'd joined had vanished into a pit of corruption. The only available job was as at a tour agency catering to older affluent North Americans .

Primping in a Benitez Airport restroom before gathering up the latest group arriving to study Chilean Nobelist Pablo Neruda's poetry and places, she re-tied the scarlet ribbons on the thick, glossy black braid men loved to unbraid and bury burning faces in, fluttered long lashes at herself, then teetered out on stilettos that made her even taller in her homeland of shortish men.

Aaaargh! There they were, slurping from water bottles, yakking loudly, behaving as if they owned Latin-America.

"Welcome to Chile! I'm Narcisa, your guide!" She flashed her professional smile. "Please have twenty dollars ready for airport tax. I'll meet you at that big blue bus outside."

As last stragglers reached the vehicle the airport shuddered. Empty trolleys slammed clankingly. Waste bins skittered. Lights fandangoed. A plump, pretty woman in a beautifully embroidered denim hat grabbed Narcias's arm, screeching in a molasses-thick Southern accent, "Mah stahs! An ay-arth-kwayik!"

"No! Just a hiccup! Chile's always burping! We warned you in our brochures, remember?" soothed Narcias, continuing to check names. As the tourist boarded the bus a thin man in faded jeans shouted hoarsely, "Hang on! Coming! Bag's still in Miami!" Limping to the steps, he stumbled up and sank into the nearest seat, gasping. It was a meeting that would be etched in the granite of Narcias's memory forever.

"Why bother sending expensive folders to gringos who never open them?" she griped to kindly Tadeo, her boss, as they bundled passports for mandatory copying by Pinochet's secret police.

"I know! But good psychology! Yanquis love handouts!"

As stocky Tadeo outlined their itinerary next morning, Narcisa stood in the doorway studying the group. Usual mix – couples who'd survived long marital wars – sprightly, well-preserved widows and divorcees – and that solo male whose bag still lingered in Miami, She'd heard him asking about it in fluent Spanish, which intrigued her since most tourists could barely mangle Gracias. Not conventionally handsome, she decided, yet attractive in a skinny sort of way. She promised herself a snoop through his passport when the ruling goons returned it.

Merlyn Caedmon Morgan, she discovered, was fifty-one, a Texan engineer who, judging by the massed visa stamps in his worn passport, had been all over South America, thus explaining his excellent Spanish. Such endless globetrotting meant he was probably unattached so, at lunch, she studied him more closely, wondering if he might be, in her parlance, "flingworthy." A new conquest might help heal the wound dealt by faithless Felipe and liven up this trip. Men, after all, must be brought to stilettoed heel.

The group rapidly split into the usual cells. Couples became quartets, single women bonded, electing Jenny Sue of the striking hat their spokeswoman. When her headgear continued drawing admiration she confided she'd embroidered it herself, adding, "If'n Ah've got to cover gray, Ah'll do it in style!" To Narcisa she later cooed, "If Ya'll didn't have such gorjus hay-ah,dah'lin, Ah'd surely love to fix Ya'll one!" A promise she would keep, though not in a way anyone could have foreseen.

Narcisa's considerable charm seemed wasted on the aloof Morgan. He began irritating Narcisa by limping more. Despite tourists being warned in advance they should be in good physical shape, she constantly had to wait for him to catch up as she shepherded her flock round Santiago's historic structures or across the tree-shaded Plaza de Armas. Only once did he open up, gently taking her mike from her after she'd given a flippant answer to yet another of Jenny Sue's inane questions, and took upon himself to explain to the appreciative group how the oddly-named Bernardo O'Higgins came to be so important in Chile's earlier turbulent history. "As if I didn't know anything!" she fumed to Tadeo later.

As the days, and her solitary nights, passed, Narcisa brooded increasingly on the obviously intelligent and well-read engineer. She would slip into the usually empty seat beside him to fish in what she suspected were the deep waters of his life but, like some cunning old trout, he always eluded her bait, making her determination to conquer escalate. As always, she never wasted thoughts on what place, if any, he might have in her life after the trip ended. Reeling him in was what mattered.

Then, with just days remaining, Narcisa became uncomfortably aware of an increasing concern for Morgan's obviously growing weariness. Her heart smote her at his disturbing breathlessness and the problem he seemed to have with swallowing. "What's wrong?" she worried. "What makes him so clumsy? He's not old-old, his hair's still thick and I'm sure those great teeth are his own!" She imagined kissing his firm mouth or exchanging the pillow-talk at which she excelled. "*Idiota!*" she would mutter before rolling over in her lumpy bed, craving the warmth she was sure he held. But, despite increasing unsteadiness and thickening speech, he waved off all concern, keeping his head turned away in the bus or pulling his hat over his eyes.

Baffled by her mounting worry and nagging concern, Narcisa hatched a scheme that could not fail to bring about Morgan's surrender.

Their final excusion was to one of Neruda's most inspirational areas, a pass nine-thousand feet up between Chile and Argentina, where recently built Las Alturas Lodge overlooked a dazzling lake. Perched on a steep bank a short distance behind it, as she well remembered, was the original, much older hotel, only used now for overbooking because so hazardous of access. Toiling up crumbling steps and across a swaying plank bridge earned a generous discount for those who had to lodge there. Now, as her weary group milled in the gleaming new lobby, Narcisa, braid touching his shoulder, leaned to whisper to Hector, the balding receptionist. At first he shook his head vehemently but, when she lightly kissed the top of it, making sweat break out, he fumbled out two keys to the old pile.

Triumphant, Narcisa moved to lobby center and lied charmingly, "Because of overbooking we've had to assign some of you to the old hotel. Because it's hard to reach we give a great discount!" Morgan, as she'd surmised he would, had collapse on to a chaise out on the patio, so missed her explanation. While Hector rolled his eyes, just as she'd also shrewdly surmised about the group, they were so relieved to be handed a key to a spanking new room they didn't linger to see who'd drawn an old one. Desperate for showers and drinks they rushed away, Jenny Sue beseeching everyone to wait for her. Swinging out to the patio, Narcisa touched Morgan gently, explained about his assignment to the older hotel and handed him one of her two special keys. Still, a pang shot through her at his drawn face and the sunken eyes usually hidden behind dark glasses. "Oh, pfft! He'll be fine after we've shared some Chilean wine!" she thought. But sharper pangs stabbed when she watched him slowly, so terribly slowly, tackling the steep steps, hauling himself hand over hand on their unsafe rail, fighting for breath. He looked so dreadfully, pitifully vulnerable that, impulsively, she called "I'd forgotten it was such a climb! If you'd rather not be up there I can get a switch!" The courageous blue stare he turned on her would haunt her down the years. He merely gasped, "No! I'm fine!"

"I'll make it up to him! I will!" Narcisa rationalized. "Then I'll confess and he'll be so flattered he'll forgive me and..." Turning away, she went to phone her daily report to Tadeo back in Santiago.

Later, a discreet number of peeling doors from Morgan's, though they were the only ones in the building, Narcisa brushed out her wait-length lustrous rope, planning to leave it loose. Excitement mounted as she imagined Morgan's surrender...and her own. She must conquer him, she must, especially after Felipe's perfidy. She hummed, spraying perfume, not noticing the golden wine in the bottle she'd set out was suddenly trembling. Only when the water in her toilet bowl sloshed over on to the floor and small wall tiles tumbled did she become aware of the growing rumble. A massive temblor sent her staggering. Her bed slid past. Plaster walls leaned inwards. She knew she must at least get under her room's lintel, wrenching her door open just as Morgan, at hall's end, wrenched his.

'Stay there!' he shouted. "I'm coming to you..." The juddering ka-boom-boom of crashing masonry drowned the rest. Enormous clouds of choking dust billowed as he began stumbling towards her, arms outstretched, across upthrust scarlet carpeting resembling bleeding gums round jagged concrete teeth that had gnawed through. Helpless, Narcisa watched Morgan vanish into a suddenly gaping hole. Every flickering light died, while water trickled eerily. She screamed and screamed until crashing debris and Stygian blackness smothered her.

Centuries later, it seemed, she crawled up from agonies in hospital, both legs in huge casts, neck in a brace. In and out of consciousness she drifted, tortured by a hideous dream in which Morgan's backward look from the broken steps was replayed endlessly while his comforting cry echoed and re-echoed. Then, late one afternoon, she opened heavy eyes to see Felipe writing on her chart, a nurse nearby.

"Oh, Felipe! Felipe! If you only knew what a wicked thing I...." Motioning her to silence he continued writing as if she'd been any patient. The setting sun gleamed on his wedding-ring. "You've been uncommonly lucky," he finally said tersely. "Not like that poor devil in the old lodge with you! By the way, the new, reinforced building held up fine except for a few cracks!" He looked down at her enigmatically before turning away.

Many pain-filled weeks later Narcisa waited in a wheelchair for Tadeo and his wife to take her home with them. From fresh habit, she passed scarred hands over her brutally shorn head, feeling its ugly stubble. "It'll grow back," said Felipe briskly, signing her discharge. "Oh, before you leave, I should tell you what Mr. Morgan's autopsy showed. Maybe make you feel a little better. Maybe not!" Again, that enigmatic look. "Seems he was suffering from Amytrophic Lateral Sclerosis – they call it Lou Gehrig's Disease in the States, after their famous baseball player who died young from it years ago. We doctors think it's perhaps the most cruel of all diseases – victims waste away, choking in the end. Horrible. Still no treatment, no cure." He paused. "Perhaps your... friend...didn't have long to live anyway. Possibly our 'quake was merciful..." He feather-touched her shoulder. "Well, here come your people. Take care!"

"Look what Jenny Sue asked me to give you!" Tadeo held out the striking hat. "She insisted! And here's a cheque too! That group took up a great collection for you, they were so concerned!"

Tremors of remorse, shudders of guilt, tsunamis of lacerating shame and utter self-loathing engulfed Narcisa. In the bustling hospital lobby she bowed her poor shaved head and wept....

Epilogue:

> *Love is so short*
> *Forgetting is so long.*
> Pablo Neruda

Reawakening
Fred Zachau
Oakdale MN

"Be out of here in half and hour."

"I'll be out in half and hour, Ed, don't push me."

"If you aren't, I'll have the cops in here to drag you out."

"Sure, Ed, you could do that, but remember this. You do, and I'll come back to get you, and what I'll do to you, you won't like at all." George, fist clenched, takes a step toward Ed, and Ed turns white.

"Just be out in half an hour," Ed says. He turns and walks down the hall to his office. George can't decide whether to laugh or continue packing or chase him and punch him out (wouldn't it be satisfying to feel his fist sink into Ed's pudgy cheek). He opts for packing. He gets everything he wants into four cardboard boxes. Eight years of corporate life into four cardboard boxes. Two years per box. The rest of the stuff in his office the janitor can throw out. George gets a hand truck and carts the boxes out to his car. He loads three of them into the trunk and the fourth onto the front seat on the passenger's side. He then returns to his office.

"Bye, Evelyn," he says to his secretary.

She hugs him. "Oh, George, I'm going to miss you."

"I'll call you in a few weeks. Linda and I are going to take you and Frank out to dinner. Okay?"

"Okay," she answers.

"And you'll be out of here in eight months, too."

"Yes." She is sixty-four and will retire in eight months.

George breaks loose and walks around to shake hands with the only four of his coworkers that he considers real friends. No long good-byes for him. He walks out to his car and begins the drive home.

"Just stay here," Linda whispers, "and for God's sake be quiet." She slips her robe over her nude body, zips it primly up to the neck, rushes out of the bedroom, shuts the door, and hurries down the stairs. She reaches the bottom just as George enters from the garage.

"Dear, you're home early," she says.

"Yeah, I'm, ah, not working this afternoon."

"Is something wrong?"

"It's a long story."

"I bet you're going to play golf."

"Well, mmm."

"You heard it's going to snow tomorrow, so you want to play one last round before winter."

"That's not a bad idea."

"I think you should."

"You do? You usually bitch when I play golf."

"You look all strung out, George. Has Ed been jerking you around at work again?"

"Yeah, Ed's been jerking me around, and Ed's a jerk, and this morning was horse shit. Maybe I should play a round all by myself."

"Sure you should. You need to relax."

"I can't believe you're encouraging me to play golf."

"I remember, George, you once said that some of the times when you felt most content you were out playing golf all by yourself."

"Yeah."

"Like those times when you used to go down and work on your sailboat and fix things that really didn't need to be fixed."

"You remember that?"

"Sure."

"Linda, we've got to talk."

"Good idea. Let's do it over dinner tonight. I'll make a pot roast."

"I've got a better idea," he says. "Let's go out to dinner. The Black Angus. Steaks and a good cabernet."

"What's up, George? You haven't offered to take me out to dinner for a year."

"That's why I think we should go out tonight. Ed's been giving me so much crap that I've been neglecting my wife."

"A filet and cabernet do sound good."

"You bet your buns, baby. And then we can talk."

"What's so important to talk about?"

"That comes tonight with the filet and cabernet."

"Okay, it's a deal. Now you'd better head for the golf course or you won't finish before dark."

George starts up the stairs toward the bedroom.

"George, where are you going?"

"To the bathroom."

"Use the one downstairs."

"Why?"

"I'm, ah, cleaning the one upstairs. The floor is wet."

As George starts for the stairs to the lower level, Linda asks, "Do you have everything you need in your locker out at the club?"

George stops at the top of the stairway, puts his hand to his forehead and thinks for a moment. "I probably should take a sweater."

"Which one do you want?"

"Oh, the green one." He continues down the stairway.

Linda rushes upstairs to the bedroom, opens a drawer, digs out a green sweater, hurries out of the bedroom without saying anything, closes the door, and runs back down to the main level. When George comes back up from the lower level, she hands it to him.

"You sure as hell seem to be in a hurry to get rid of me."

"George, I'm not. It's just that it gets dark early now. You'll only be able to get in nine, you know."

"I know. Hey, Linda, do you know whose car that is across the street?" he asks pointing to a white Ford Taurus with a small dent in the left front fender."

She looks out the window. "No."

"Seems to me I've seen it before," George says.

"There are a lot of white Fords on the road now."

"Yeah, but this one has a dent in the left front fender. I'm sure I've seen it before, but I can't remember where."

"Maybe Bill bought another car."

"I haven't heard that he did. I'll have to ask him."

"I don't think it's anything to worry about," Linda says.

"Maybe not. I'd better get going. I wonder if I should call ahead for a tee time."

"You shouldn't need one this late in the season on a Wednesday afternoon."

"I guess not." George picks up his sweater and starts for the door to the garage. "Linda, will you make a six-thirty reservation for us at the Black Angus?"

"Sure. Have a good round."

George looks at her quizzically. "Thanks. You know, your hair is all mussed up."

"I've been working, George."

"What kind of work."

"Cleaning the bathroom, remember?"

"Oh, that's right. You know, you look kind of cute with your hair like that. Maybe I should forget about golf and,"

"No!" She interrupts, throws up her hands, then relaxes. "I just mean let's wait until after dinner. You know how I get after a couple glasses of wine."

"Yeah," he says, leering. "This day might not be so bad after all. Golf, dinner, wine, and, heh, heh. After dinner I shall carry thee off to my chambers and hold thee prisoner to be my playmate."

"And I shall fight thee off with a noodle from my pasta salad."

George jumps back. "What, fair lady, must a knight do to win thy favors?"

"Bring me back a scorecard proving you broke a bogey round."

"Done!" he cries.

Linda giggles. "Get thee to the golf course," she commands, pointing.

"Yes, ma'am." He enters the garage and closes the door. Three seconds later the door opens about ten inches and George's head, which normally resides six feet and two inches above the floor, appears at the level of Linda's knees. "See you later," the head says. Another leer. The door closes again.

Linda walks to the front window and watches George back the car out of the driveway, turn left, and vanish down the street. Balls, that was close. Damn that white Taurus. Harry has to get that dent fixed right away. Got to get Harry out of here pronto. But why is George being so nice to me? He actually paid attention to me. Tried to make me laugh. Those last few moments with him were fun, really fun, like it used to be. We haven't clowned around like that since—she can't remember. What's happening? Are things going to change? Is there still a chance? She crosses the room and slowly climbs the stairs to the bedroom. She does not think about sex. Instead she wonders, What should I wear to dinner tonight?

The first hole on the Crestview Country Club golf course is a 368-yard sharp dogleg to the left. George's tee shot starts out straight down the middle. Then it begins to hook slightly left. Perfect, he thinks, right around the dogleg. But the hook deepens and the ball heads toward the big red pine at the apex of the dogleg. "My favorite tree," groans George aloud. The ball strikes the trunk of the red pine and bounces back into the middle of the fairway leaving him with an easy five-iron shot. If he hadn't hit the tree, he would have had an easier seven-iron, but a five-iron isn't bad. Maybe this is a good day, he speculates. Usually when he hits that tree the ball ricochets left into the deep woods never to be seen again. George pushes the driver into his bag and walks down the fairway pondering his life.

How stupid he's been to let Ed and that job make him miserable for, what, maybe five years now. He should have quit and told Ed to go to hell five years ago. He can always get another job. Maybe he won't make quite as much money, but it will be good enough. Has it really been a year since he took Linda out to dinner? He's been so obsessed with building a career that he forgot why he wanted to build it. And he's been rotten to Linda. He's treated her as if she were in the way of the career. He recalls a line from a song: "To die for a cause they've long ago forgotten." Okay, he's finally remembered why he wanted the career in the first place. It's time to change things. Tonight he'll start working on it. If only it isn't too late. Please, God, don't let it be too late.

He stops, pulls his five-iron out of his bag, stands about ten feet back from the ball, and lines up the shot. He takes a practice swing. Then he addresses the ball just like Tiger Woods does it. It's a good day. It's going to be a good shot. He can feel it.

* * *

John Hildebidle
Cambridge MA

So Close

Summers, his idea of a family trip
was for the three of us to make the rounds
of customers in towns we'd never heard of:
Ypsilanti, Sioux Falls, Downer's Grove, Gary.
The worst times were when Mom and I
sat parked in the sun while he was inside
seeing to his mysterious business.
On the road, at least there was air.
In the old vast Buick, measured mile signs
Brought as much delight as Burma Shave ads,
Howard Johnson's. All attention, terrified
I'd miss the one saying "Measured mile begins NOW" –
then I'd start counting seconds,
"one Mississippi, two Mississippi, three. . ."
At the finish, I'd total up, run the math,
peeking over Dad's shoulder. "Speedometer's a bit off.
Better have it checked, when we get home."
"Roger. Ten four." All that responsibility!"

Louise Norman
Tullahoma TN

Music Nights at 24th and Dixie

Our music trickles through
the summer night
as we play and sing
in the house at
24th and Dixie Place.

Light pools on the piano keys,
leaving sheet music in half-shadow.
Aunt Irene's true soprano soars
pure and clear above
the thumps of my playing
as the canary flings out
an obbligato.

Alto notes tumble out of my mouth
like water pouring from
the backyard faucet.
The music flows out
the open windows and doors,
sending ripples of sound
to neighbors sitting
on their porches.

I have the freedom to
wander at will in the
world, but I miss the house
at 24th and Dixie;
long for the neighborhood of
big, old houses nestled
between Vanderbilt and Peabody College;
lost now to the VA Hospital
and parking lots.

I yearn for the warm
summer weeks spent with
grandmother and aunt;
teachers of my childhood,
keepers of the music.

"Broken In Weber Creek"

by Stephen Figler
Cambria CA

Honest John Nagengast awoke with his face in Weber Creek or Hangman's Creek, he couldn't figure out which. His lungs ached, either from the absence of air or the presence of water, couldn't figure that out either. He knew his head was below water because it was numb with the cold of the snow-melt water and because he could see the swirls of his own blood carried past his eyes in the otherwise crystalline water.

The main thing was, he couldn't figure out whether it was worth lifting his head the few inches to get his nose and mouth above the water. He was half dead already, which didn't seem so bad compared to what life had been these past six months panning for gold, protecting his claim, avoiding fights with men for whom fighting seemed their reason for breathing. And there was the pining for a woman. That had gotten so bad almost any woman would do. But you had to go down to the flatlands to Sutter's Town to get your hands on one, which meant leaving your claim, so to hell with it. To hell with it all. He wondered how long he could last without air.

Tools, that was the problem, not enough to go around, which was how he got in the water, or rather why. A problem for himself and the growing horde of miners, tools and supplies. Back home in Springfield, it would be the most mundane of trials, a matter of a few dollars. Here in the Gold Rush in this crowded yet unserved west, it was the problem which, if a man failed, nothing else mattered.

Food was easy. Jack-rabbit, squirrel, turkey, if you could conserve powder and shot. Crayfish and trout, if you could find hook and line. Fig trees and blackberries teemed along the creeks, although you could find yourself shitting away half the day if you didn't govern consumption.

Honest John's lungs no longer ached. Nor his skull where the pickaxe creased it. The blood was a thin trickle in the current passing his eyes. He no longer missed the air just inches away.

Tools were hardest to come by and he'd awakened that morning to find his new pickax gone, bought just the day before at the Round Tent in Dry Diggins. He'd propped it against a bull-pine, slid into his bedroll, wakened with the sun in his eyes, stirred the night's oak coals and added some dry manzanita twigs, gone down to the creek-side for a pot of water, come back and dropped in coffee beans when he'd sensed something wasn't right, turned and saw the pickax was gone. Which was how he'd gotten into this pickle, looking up from the bottom of an icy creek.

Past pain Honest John saw through the inches of water a solitary cloud, or maybe it was a last bubble from his lungs and out a mouth he couldn't feel anymore.

He had been panning at the confluence of Weber and Hangman's Creeks just beyond where the latter tumbled down a 100-foot high staircase of brown rock. When the pickax creased his skull, it must have happened on the Weber Creek side of the Y, a fact about to lose import unless they cared about such detail wherever it was his s—oul was about to go.

He was Weber Creek now, or close to being Weber Creek, like a water-carved boulder or a pine snag or the crumbled shell of a crayfish. No difference between him and anything else between the banks.

The Arkansawyer—younger, taller, stronger, meaner—had stepped from behind a pile of rock tossed over the months from the creek to form a sluicing channel. He was holding a new green pickax like a rifle at port arms. Before Honest John could say Howdy or That's a mighty fine tool you're holding, the Arkansawyer said, "This hyere's mahn."

"Like hell it is," said Honest John, taking the man's insistence in the absence of question as an admission of guilt. It would have been so in Missouri, and no reason to feel otherwise in the California gold fields. He stepped forward to take back his property, for which he'd paid seven dollars.

For weapons all Honest John had were his his wits, which were no match for a well-swung pickax employed by an angry Arkansawyer. Which he realized from beneath the water was the point: not enough pickaxes to go around.

Which led Honest John to decide that he wasn't ready to die. He lifted his face from the water and fought his dormant lungs to make them return to work. The sky turned black, then a brilliant white, then black again, then white. A fist inside his chest pounded trying to break out. He tried to inhale, but his lungs were filled with icy mountain water.

Honest John rolled to his hands and knees. Midnight rapidly approached, foregoing dusk and evening. Stars, larger than he'd ever seen, floating before his eyes. Two fresh jerky slabs in his pack. Shameful waste. More's the shame if the damned Arkansawyer got to eat them. He could stand up. Maybe he could stand. He willed his knees to straighten, then his back. He tottered and looked around, not knowing what he was looking for, only that his lungs were stiff, rigid, not behaving. He rotated a quarter turn, saw a round-top boulder poking above the water. He toppled across it like a felled tree, the contents of his lungs gushing out.

* * *

A gray crawdad nibbled at Honest John's fingers. He was draped like a pile of wash over a boulder. He flicked and the crawdad scuttled away. His ribs ached like he'd been mule-kicked. Which was a good thing, because, as the saying goes, the dead feel no pain. The water's surface rippled close below his face, which was progress because minutes, hours, maybe a day ago, his face had been below that surface. He lapped like a dog. Near drowned and now he had the cotton mouth.

He pushed away from the rock onto his knees and coughed pink foam into the moving water. With each spasm, the fist slammed his chest. Honest John touched his breastbone lightly with the tips of two fingers, felt a sharp agony that paled the pain from deeper within. The breast bone was dented, maybe shattered. He'd done it to himself, survived the Arkansawyer's head blow followed by near drowning, only to crush his own breast. Although if he hadn't forced the water from his lungs by falling on the boulder, he'd've drowned in the bone-dry California air.

A quick death compared to this, and all over a pickax. With the money tucked up in his pants, he could've bought 10 pickaxes, 20, more, even at Comstock's unconscionable price. But Comstock had come up from Sutter's Fort with only one pickax and a wagon-load of blankets in August, and none of the promised and longed-for butter and other provisions. Every two weeks Comstock brought what he couldn't sell in the valley.

A band of sunlight cut across the top of Green Valley ridge to the south. Dusk was coming. He turned gingerly. At the north shore treeline, not bothering to hide, four coyotes eyed him, no, five. He'd be safe from them for the night if he stayed in the water, but he'd die of exposure, the cold wind sure to roll downslope from the high country through Weber Canyon.

And there were the cougars. Only way to be safe from them was with a rifle or a campfire. He didn't own the former and wasn't up to gathering wood to make the latter, even if he could find a dry match. There was a settlement of panners upstream about a mile. A mile to walk, or more likely stumble, half dead and spitting blood, cold to his marrow in the boulder-strewn stream, the canyon bottom already losing its ridge-blocked, tree-filtered light.

The settlement had a thousand men, tents for the well-healed, lean-to's for the ambitious, a spot on the ground for the uncommitted. Called The Tubs because of the shallow waterfall and the two calm, water-carved basins below it. The upstream one was used by the men for bathing. The other, separated only by a flat boulder was reserved for women, though no human female to anyone's memory had ever been in it. Wishful thinking of the men, but then what was panning for gold?

Weber Creek had no proper bank like the rivers back home in Missouri. Honest John had to make his way up stream in the water, the sharp stabs in his chest vanquishing even the throb throughout his head. Over-hanging limbs, thickets of thorny blackberry, and wiry stands of poison oak spread beyond the creek's edge. Pain above, numb from the cold below. He could barely feel the stony creek-bed through his boots, fought to maintain momentum over slick and unsettled rock.

The sun sank beneath the ridge line, the air quickly thickening. Darkness would soon be profound.

Ahead, a small rapid curled around a knee-high boulder. In the half light of a purpling sky the boulder looked to be basin-topped. Honest John lifted a leg high from the swirling water, planted his boot on the boulder, and leaned forward to climb. He reached a hand down for balance, found a shallow puddle of warm water in the boulder's depression, and felt the slime, too late. He was most of the way up when the boot began to slip. He tottered, then tilted backwards. A flailing hand hit a tree limb. He grabbed it and held. His broken breastbone separated. He shrieked, the torment so engulfing, his brain couldn't tell the hand to let go of the bending branch until he was ass-down in the swirling water.

The coyotes answered Honest John's shriek with a volley of their own hoots, howls, and yips. A rifle cracked from the settlement up at The Tubs, momentarily silencing the coyotes and reducing Honest John to a whimper. The men would be firing into the dark at sounds. And words—Don't shoot; I'm hurt—would not travel near as far as rifle balls.

He refrained from hugging himself because the warmth would pale next to the pain from his broken bones. He coughed and moaned from the jolt and felt the foam from his lungs rise through throat to mouth. He tasted the tang of diluted blood. He spat into the stream, coughed, moaned, and spat again.

There was no doctor at The Tubs. Nor, last he'd heard, up at Dry Diggins, the gathering of tents that had become an actual town within months of the gold strike. The best he could hope for was someone who'd suffered a chest injury like his and figured out how to survive, or someone who knew Miwok medicine. There was one thing to be thankful for. The Arkansawyer could have hit him with the point of the pickax instead of the flat.

* * *

"Weber Creek, Hangman's Creek, them ain't so populous as the American and the Cosumnes, which are the full-bore rivers hereabouts," the one-toothed man mucking out Borelli's Stables had said when John Nagengast first arrived in

Dry Diggins, with his good-for-nothing mule. Although it was that mule made him "Honest John," so maybe the thing had been good for something. He'd picked up the mule at the new town on the river they were calling Sacramento, growing so fast it would soon surround Sutter's Fort. He'd named the mule Mercury out of blind, dumb hope, as if the beast would honor the mythical origin of its new moniker. In the contrary nature of its kind, the mule turned out to be the slowest four-legged brute he had ever encountered, not that he'd had all that much to do with the lower forms of animal life back in Springfield.

He'd just spent six months sailing by fast packet around Cape Horn. They'd been lucky, nearly everyone said, the whole trip stormless and benefitting from good winds, then passing the mingling of the Atlantic and Pacific waters with no more than several hard lists to starboard. Most of the hundred or so 49ers on board took the mild weather and the winds as good omens, signs that they were destined to strike it rich in the gold fields of the Sierra Nevada. A few saw their calm passing around the cape as a bad sign, depletion of their allotment of luck.

"God damned waste," said a coal miner from Hazleton, Pennsylvania, the creases of his thick face, neck, and hands still bearing the black of his trade months after his last descent into the earth. "A man's luck runs out quicker'n he can drown a daisy in piss," he said. "No sense awastin' it on agettin' where you're agoin'. Druther hold onto my luck 'till I get there."

His name was Moyer and he had run up the gangplank in New Orleans just as the deckhands were about to unleash it. Moyer began his complaining before the duffel bag swung from his shoulder and hit the deck.

The other 49ers swarming the deck of the packet had initially moved away from Moyer, not welcoming negativity at that particular moment of their lives. Then Moyer began to talk about mining, and like a neap tide, the men closed around him. Most of them had left lives as store clerks or dirt farmers or scriveners or sausage makers and such. John Nagengast had been a newspaper writer. Gold mining was what they had turned their lives toward, and here aboard their boat was a genuine miner talking his trade. No matter that mining coal in the earth's bowels had as much to do with gold panning in rivers as slaughtering a chicken has to do with frying it. Still, even John Nagengast found himself drawing nigh to listen to Moyer ramble on about Mother Earth's jealousy of her jewels.

"She'll give up her foodstuffs easy enough," Moyer said. A note or three of dispute was sounded by those farmers gathered on deck. Moyer grumbled back at them. "Old Mother Earth knows enough to feed the fools who tickle and trim her. Like all dames, she relish's worship. But those of us who have the mettle to penetrate her, dig deep for her treasures, her jewels, well, we need our luck if we expect to live long enough to spend our booty. Can't be frivoling luck away on agreeable weather."

John Nagengast looked around the crowd of soon to be gold prospectors listening to Moyer. They sat on haunches or rope coils or leaned against the ship's rail or lay on hatch covers under the cold, starry sky, by now all of them adapted to the tilt of the deck, if not its rolling. He'd done some reading on the kind of gold mining being done in the California hills. The newer kind was hydraulic mining conducted by large companies, blasting away at hillsides with water canons, then sluicing out the heavier gold from the dirt and rock tailings. In the smaller streams and creeks men still placer mined, panning out grains and flakes and the occasional small nugget. That's what most of the men like them, independent souls, would be doing. In the frigid winter night near the tip of Argentina, listening to the coal miner named Moyer prattle on about mining gold, John Nagengast felt compelled to say something to the men.

"Mr. Moyer's knowledge about extracting Mother Earth's jewels is based on his experience with coal, tunnel mining. Few of us will be doing that once we arrive at the gold fields. Furthermore, I have some difficulty with Mr. Moyer's metaphor. I, for one, am hard-pressed to view a lump of coal as a jewel which Mother Earth, would jealously protect."

"Ha!" said Moyer in a heart-beat. "Show's how much you know with all your book-learnin'. In time that lump of black coal will be a crystal clear diamond, and what's Mother Earth got more of than time, hey, Bub? Answer me that, scribbler."

Moyer was right to a point. John Nagengast shut his mouth, although his point had not been the jewel metaphor, but the method of mining, which Moyer was no more privy to than the rest of them.

John Nagengast grew the "Honest" appendage onto his name when he arrived in the community once called Dry Diggins but recently renamed Hangtown for good reason. What he did to earn the title was refuse Dante Borelli's offer of the full price of one hundred dollars for the mule he had mis-named Mercury. The owner of a new lumber mill several miles upslope from Hangtown had been badgering Borelli for an eight-mule team. Borelli was one mule shy when Mercury ambled into his stables with John Nagengast aboard.

Mules were for carrying, not riding, John Nagengast had been informed by the man who'd sold him the beast at Sutter's Fort. But after weeks on the ocean, his feet had gone soft, and after walking 20 miles east into the foothills in brand new boots, John Nagengast wished he didn't own feet. So he climbed onto Mercury for the last 15 or so miles, the rules of mule-tending be damned. But Mercury must have known those rules, because she'd stand stock still for hours on end, only sauntering on when Providence or some stray scent moved her.

"I'd be pleased to buy your mule for one hundred dollars," Borelli said to

Nagengast, who was at that moment contemplating the removal of every one of his ten toes to allay the torment of several blisters on each of them. The new boots he'd bought in San Francisco were thick and heavy, "for the trials of the high country," the salesman had told him. Another customer at the bootery on Market Street, a man with the demeanor of well-earned knowledge, had warned John Nagengast to soak the boots and let them dry on his feet whilst standing at a saloon bar or some other venue that allowed time to pass pleasantly. But John Nagengast, like most people, failed to attach value to free advice. Besides, there was no time, the paddle-wheeler leaving for Sutter's Fort in less than an hour and the business of his last civilized whore to get done before the boat departed. And so the mule and his blisters.

To Borelli's offer, John Nagengast said, "Mine is a defective mule. She's strong enough, but stubborn and slow. I named her Mercury, but Molasses would be more apt. I cannot in good conscience take more than eighty dollars for her."

Word spread quicker than the croup at a schoolhouse within the tent community of Dry Diggins, instantly earning John Nagengast the sobriquet of "Honest." Though he'd never cheated a soul that he knew of, in fact had been cheated more than in his purchase of Mercury, as well as by his too-pretty wife back in Missouri, he could not recall ever having been singled out for probity. He liked the name and when introducing himself, began to use it. He became Honest John Nagengast of Springfield, Missouri, without pausing to reflect that it had ever not been a part of his name.

* * *

Honest John moved up Weber Creek more now by sound than by sight. He could smell the smoke of campfires wafting downslope along the creek bed with the cool night breeze. Yellow light flickered in the limbs and on the hillsides, but the light at such distance offered no illumination.

He had begun to sense the presence of boulders in his path by the swirl of waters around them. Over the rush he heard the crackle and scurry of animals along the shore and birds leaving branches as he approached. A mourning dove cooed up one of the hillsides, whether from the south or north, it was difficult to tell because of the tricks of sound in a canyon.

The pain spreading outward from his chest had not subsided, although he seemed acclimated. It had become the normalcy of his life, as marriage and family once had been. As church had been. As seeking stories and writing daily for the weekly Bugle had been. Now excruciating pain was normalcy, his job, his religion. Honest John Nagengast was now married to his pain.

He wondered what might have been his lot had he not listened to the one-toothed man at Borelli's Stable. He might have gone to the American River or the Cosumnes, where there were more gold seekers and, while perhaps less chance of finding sufficient gold, at least more of what passed for civilization, less chance of getting skulled by a desperate Arkansawyer. Instead, he took the man's advice and went to the creeks. But what if he'd taken the Hangman's branch instead of the Weber branch? Would he have avoided getting brained and broken? Might some other misery have awaited him? Can a man avoid his fate? Swinging a leg slowly over a downed and bark-stripped tree trunk, Honest John thought not.

Light flickered brighter through the branches. A campfire. Two. Three. The outermost of the community sprung up at The Tubs. It had taken him four, maybe five hours to trek the mile from where the Arkansawyer had struck him down. But with help in sight, his legs were giving out. His thigh muscles quivered with the effort of lifting each leg through the water. His knees creaked with each step, seeming to need the services of an oil can. The muscles of his lower stomach felt knotted like ship's hawsers. And there was his chest, the broken, perhaps irreparable part of him.

Honest John stumbled around a bend in the creek, the sound of the lower waterfall of The Tubs rising as if a window in some house in some city had been opened to street noise. He raised a leg achingly onto a sloping shore of sand and sunk to hands and knees. He drew a couple of short draughts of air before crawling toward a lean-to of boughs propped against a pair of close-growing pines.

"I'm Honest John Nagen...," he called out, the last of his name dying in a croak. He gathered himself. "A man hurt and in dire need of help."

The fire ring a yard or so from the lean-to held a small flame above a glowing bed of embers. He heard a stirring from inside the lean-to, then a man emerged, unfolding to a lanky height. Honest John knew the harsh curl of mouth. It was the Arkansawyer, who reached for the pickax leaning against one of the pines.

The breath ebbed from Honest John's breast. Against his pain, he drew in another and said, "Tell me this at least, sir. Is that thing truly yours or mine?"

*[This story is Chapter Two from **Hangtown**, a novel of the Gold Rush.*
Also, a version of the story won a scholarship to
the Art of the Wild Writers' Conference, Squaw Valley, California.]

Three Simple Words
By Thomas E. Barisano
Newtonville, Ma

My father was a meat-and-potatoes kind of guy. He liked to watch football and boxing on TV, especially two big heavyweights duking it out in the ring. He expressed his love for his wife and three sons mainly through his ability to feed, clothe, and shelter them. The closest he'd ever come to telling me that he loved me was on rare occasions when he'd said, "Your mother and I both love you very much." Even then, the words had stumbled past his lips with all the grace of bumper cars. But it was not the form that mattered to me, it was the substance and the knowledge that such sentiment from him was almost as rare as a snowstorm in July.

I, too, was guilty. A victim, as my father was, of upbringing and society. Actions spoke louder than words anyway, right? Well, perhaps, but there came a time when you wanted to go beyond the mere actions, beyond that tacit understanding, and beyond those Christmas, birthday, and Father's Day cards and utter aloud those three simple words.

In September of 1990 my dad was diagnosed with inoperable pancreatic cancer. Two-and-a-half months later, after weeks of chemotherapy and the painful process of watching a rotund, 250-pound human being waste helplessly away, the telephone in my condo rang at around ten o'clock one Tuesday morning. It was the call I'd hoped would never come.

"Thomas," my mother's sweet voice trembled into the receiver, and before she'd spoken another word I knew what she was going to say next, "it's your father," she said. "He's very bad. He couldn't even stay up to watch Monday Night Football. The hospice nurse was just here. She doesn't expect him to make it through the day."

"Okay. Calm down. Relax." I said, trying to be strong for her—for me. "do Steve and Richie know?"

"I called them at work." Her voice trembled again. "They're on their way."

"I'll be there as soon as I can."

The six mile drive from Brookline to Newton seemed to take forever that morning. Could things get any worse, I wondered? First I get laid off from my job, then this. Usually, whenever I drove in my car, my radio or cassette player would be turned on and pounding out my favorite music. But that day it seemed like a useless toy and silence prevailed. Instead, despite the colorful splendor of a cool, crisp, sun-bathed morning in the middle of November, I felt like I was driving in some long, dark, quiet tunnel.

When I arrived, I parked my red Topaz alongside the curb in front of the dark brown brick buildings of the Horace Mann Elderly Apartments, and for a few minutes I sat staring out my windshield, part of me wanting to rush right in, part of me not wanting to go in at all.

When I finally did, I discovered ma down on one knee disinfecting the toilet bowl with a white-bristled brush, both arms immersed halfway to her elbows in bright yellow rubber gloves. I figured I'd find her that way—cleaning. Or baking. Or both. That's what she did whenever something was bothering her. I suppose it provided some form of therapy or diversion, or again, perhaps both. Today I surmised I'd eat well in a very clean apartment. "Hi, Ma." I said, announcing my arrival as I stood just outside the small, blue-tiled bathroom which adjoined the bedroom. "How's Dad?" I asked, placing a tentative glance at him quietly sleeping in his big, king-sized bed, a nice cream-colored blanket covering him up to his chin.

For a moment, she stopped her incessant scrubbing and looked up at me with those loving, chocolate-brown eyes of hers. "The hospice nurse left a little while ago." She said, shaking her gray-haired head dubiously back and forth. "His pulse is real weak. She doesn't expect him to make it through the day."

I wanted to be strong for her, like on the telephone, but deep inside me there was a little boy who didn't know what to say or how to react. I wasn't sure what I wanted to do more—scream or cry, or what bothered me the most, the fact that my father was probably going to die today, or that my mother was finally willing to accept it. She might have been, but I wasn't.

"How the heck does she know!" I protested. "They can be wrong, can't they?"

"They know, Thomas." Ma replied, returning to her therapeutic scrubbing. "They see this sort of thing every day." Then she repeated what she'd told me on the telephone about him not being able to watch Monday Night Football, adding emphatically, "I had to call for a delivery of morphine last night the pain was so bad—and you know your father."

Yes, I knew my father, and for him not staying up to watch Monday Night Football was bad enough, but when she told me about the morphine, well, let's just say that's when I knew it was serious. Since the whole awful ordeal had begun back in September, I could never so much as recall a single moan or groan out of him. Oh sure, when he was alone, he probably did. And then there were those occasions when he'd be sitting in his easy chair reading or watching TV, and suddenly he'd stop and gaze down at the floor or up at the ceiling for a moment. I never said anything, nor did he, but I knew those were the times he was experiencing tremendous levels of pain.

"Then this morning he wouldn't wake up." Ma said, struggling to her feet now ". So I called the nurse. She came right over. We cleaned him up. That's when she told me his pulse was weak, and she didn't expect him to make it through the day."

As Ma spoke, my eyes wandered over to my father once again. He looked so peaceful, head propped up on two, big feather pillows, eyes tightly shut, his thin silver-gray hair with the tiny circular bald spot in the middle, neatly combed. I just couldn't believe how fast the cancer had transformed a once strong, plump-faced, pot-bellied man, and in only ten weeks turned him into such a gaunt, bony-faced human being who could hardly stand up anymore or speak.

I shook my head. I sighed. I never thought it would come to this. Even though, back in September when the oncologist had gathered us all together in one room at the hospital and behind closed doors told us point-blank that he was probably going to die from this, I refused to believe it. He's sick, I told myself. He'll get better. The doctors will cure him. The family will pray. If needed, a miracle would happen—but he'll be fine.

As I did then, I still believed in miracles now.

Fenway Park, October, 1967.

My Dad was a big Red Sox fan. I was, too. In 1967, after two decades of mediocre seasons and near last place finishes, they won the American League pennant. But it wasn't easy. That year, by the time the final weekend of the season rolled around, four teams still had a shot at it. All the Sox had to do was beat Minnesota on Saturday and Sunday and hope Detroit lost one of its three remaining games.

Somehow Dad got his hands on a pair of tickets to Saturday's game. We sat on the third base side just behind the visitor's dugout and two rows back from the box seats. Heaven on earth to a pimple-faced fifteen-year-old and a pot-bellied, balding, middle-aged man.

Fenway was beautiful that day. The air was cool and crisp, and the infield dirt glimmered like polished oakwood nestled amid a sea of deep green, perfectly manicured blades of grass. And overhead, the sky loomed, a cloudless, crystal-clear cobalt-blue dome.

But by the fifth inning, the wondrous splendor that surrounded us seemed destined to be marred by a painful, season-ending loss. The Sox trailed 2-0. Then, in the bottom of the inning with two runners on, Carl Yastrzemski strode to the plate. That year, Yastrzemski had been the team's guiding force, and he would eventually capture the triple crown.

"C'mon Yaz!" I shouted, as he dug in.

The first two pitches sailed outside the strike zone. Then, on the next pitch, Yaz took a mighty swing and connected. In unison, 33,000 people leaped to their feet, and a tense hush took temporary possession of 66,000 hopeful, watching, waiting eyes.

The Minnesota right fielder raced back until the squat wall some 380 feet from homeplate would give him no more ground, and with a desperate, valiant leap attempted to snare the now rapidly descending white sphere in his outstretched glove. But, as he'd done forty-three times before that season, Yaz had struck the ball too well, and it came to rest in the Red Sox bullpen instead for a three-run homer.

The hush, like a lit fuse that had finally reached its point of detonation, erupted into a deafening roar as Yaz, brimming now with a proud, triumphant grin, rounded the bases receiving a vigorous handshake from coach Eddie Popowski as he trotted past third.

Next to me, above the endless, jubilant din, my dad's lone voice somehow managed to stand out. For a moment, it was as if it was the only voice that existed, and when I glanced over at him I was amazed at what I saw. He was jumping up and down and clapping his chubby little hands together like an excited little boy and squealing, "Yea! Yea! Yea!"

That was baseball. It brought out the kid in all of us, even the strong, silent, meat-and-potatoes types like my father. He'd waited a long time for this. I had, too. Everyone had. And as I stood there cheering and going wild like everyone else, I knew this was a moment I'd never forget. (For the record, the Sox went on to win the game. On Sunday, they won as well, and when the Tigers split a double-header in Detroit, the Red Sox captured their first American League pennant in many years.)

The afternoon of November thirteenth was filled with a constant, intermittent flow of friends and relatives in and out of the small apartment. As I had suspected, ma baked and cleaned all day and spent a lot of time on the telephone, both making and receiving calls as the news of dad's worsening condition spread.

At one o'clock, the hospice nurse returned. Her stay was brief. First thing she did was call her office. Then she took off her feathery overcoat and marched unaccompanied into the bedroom, closing the hollow particle board door securely behind her.

"He's quite a fighter.:" She remarked, when she emerged a few minutes later. "When I left this morning, I didn't think he'd make it past noon." She added, sounding more like she was talking about what was on sale at the local supermarket rather than a human being's life. Good Lord, I felt like screaming! Show some respect will you lady! That's my Dad you're talking about! The man who's loved and cared for me for the past thirty-nine years.

Then I remembered ma's words from this morning about how these people saw this sort of thing every day. To them it was just a part of their job like a gas station attendant who pumped your gas, or a trash collector who picked up your trash. Still though, I felt resentful.

Like I said, her stay had been brief. Fifteen minutes, if that. At the front door, she gave ma a consoling hug and told her she'd be back later on unless something happened in the meantime. In that case, she was to contact her immediately on her cellphone, and she'd return as promptly as she could. Then she donned her coat and was gone.

Sammy White's bowling alley, circa 1960.

During the colder months of the year, after Sunday dinner, Dad would take me to Sammy White's, a local bowling alley about five miles from where we lived. It was kind of a tradition with us, although some days I was sure he would have preferred to just plunk himself down in his easy chair and watch football. But he knew how much I looked forward to it, so he always took me.

One Sunday the place was a madhouse. It was usually busy on Sundays, but on this particular afternoon it was especially jampacked. People milled about everywhere, and the air was hot and smelled of cigarette smoke and alley wax, and I could hear the usual, constant clattering of pins and the periodic outbursts of cheers and jeers and laughter from those lucky enough to have gotten an alley. All forty lanes were in use.

"How long a wait?" Dad asked the young man behind the tall, white formica counter.

"Could be an hour or more." He promptly informed us.

"Okay." Dad said, after considering for a moment. "Gimme a tag." (A tag was a quarter-sized, metal object with a number from 1-40 embossed on it. When you heard this number announced over the P.A. system, that meant it was your turn to bowl.)

Alas, two hours, five or so coffee-flavored frappes, some odd-number of cheeseburgers later, and with many tag numbers yet to be called before ours, we were still waiting. Finally my dad's patience ran out. "Come on, Thomas!" He grumbled. "I think I've had about enough of this!" And with that, thus began an angry march toward the front desk, interrupted only by a quick stop at the coat rack.

"What the hell kinda place you runnin'" here!" He hollered, as he slammed the metal tag down hard onto the white formica counter. "Me and my kid been waitin' over two damn hours!" He ranted, not ashamed who else might hear. "What the hell you doin' givin' all the open alleys to your buddies!"

The man behind the counter immediately flung both hands up over his head as if to proclaim his innocence. "I'm sorry, sir," he apologized, " it's just very busy today."

"Sure it is!" Dad snarled, as he stormed away, charging through the spacious Plexiglas doors like a raging bull. "Come on, Thomas!" He rumbled. "Let's get the hell outa here!"

Disappointed, I ran to catch up, and as the glass doors closed behind me the din of the bowling alley quickly gave way to the soothing whisper of a cold yet sunny late fall afternoon. In the parking lot, still muttering angrily beneath his breath, dad searched among a sea of cars for our black Dodge Dart.

Sure, I knew he'd probably been wrong to holler at the guy and accuse him as he did. I think, deep down, he'd known that, too. But That was my dad, always the type to blow off steam first and ask questions later. I'll admit, I'd felt a bit embarrassed at the time—guilty, too. After all, if not for me he could have been home sitting in his nice comfortable easy chair watching football.

By five o'clock, the sparkling mid-November sunlight had dwindled from the sky and the small apartment, like the world outside, grew subdued and quiet. Even dad's precious TV sat resting atop its squat mahogany table down at the center end of the living room, blank and quiet now, too. How he'd loved his TV. Sometimes, I'd wondered, maybe as much as the animate members of his family. That, and his easy chair situated just a few feet in front of it. A chair whose nap had been worn away from its back, seat, and arms and whose off-white upholstery had been soiled so badly from body oil, sweat, and newspaper ink that it had turned a sort of blackish-white now from the multitude of years that he'd spent residing in it, especially since retiring fourteen years ago. I swear, he must've sat there watching his TV from 8 AM till midnight, nonstop some days.

Aside from sports, his two favorite shows were *The Price Is Right* and *Wheel of Fortune*. I suppose he derived some sort of vicarious satisfaction out of watching other people win lavish prizes and large sums of money.

In his day, he'd done his share of gambling. Cards. The horses. Numbers. In later years, the lottery. Ma told me once that he blew the rent money at the race track one night. She said she almost left him, but he promised it would never happen again. It didn't. I was still in diapers then.

But I guess you had to understand, he was just an ordinary joe, my dad. When he was a boy, he'd told me on more than one occasion, he'd had to go to work at a local paper mill after school so his family could make ends meet. That was how he'd spent his whole life—struggling, trying to make ends meet. Gambling to him had not been a sickness but a way—the only way, he felt he'd ever be able to strike it rich. The only way he'd ever be able to give his three sons and the woman he'd married and loved so deeply everything they'd ever wanted—and more.

Now all I wanted was to see him sitting in that soiled, beat-up old easy chair watching his TV again. Or maybe, more accurately, slouched down in it half asleep, a wad of sugarless gum lodged between his slack, unmoving lips while he snored merrily away.

Throughout that long, difficult afternoon, I trekked in and out of the bedroom many times. Each time I'd massaged his stiff, motionless feet poking up beneath the clean, cream-colored blanket like two little mountains. Somehow I yearned to comfort him, to communicate with him. I wanted him to know that we were all there, his three sons and loving, dedicated wife with whom he'd shared life's ups and downs for the past forty-nine years. I didn't know if he could feel my touch, but I did know he could hear my voice because the hospice nurse told ma that when a person was dying their hearing was the last thing to go.

So I spoke to him, too. I said things like, "We're all pulling for you, dad. Hang in there. You're gonna get better." And, "Hey, the Patriots are looking pretty good this year." But the one thing I really wanted to say, I hadn't.

Then at around 4 PM I entered the bedroom making sure the particle board door was firmly shut behind me. As usual, I massaged his motionless feet. As usual, there was no response. So I stepped quietly to one side of the big double bed and gazed down at him, at that pale, shrunken face, and for an instant I thought I was going to cry, but I didn't.

His breathing had become increasingly more infrequent now, having done so with each passing hour. And whenever he did breathe, it was an ugly, grating gasp to draw air into a pair of rapidly failing lungs. It was called the death rattle, at least according to the bluntly phrased words of the hospice nurse.

Finally, I was ready. In my chest my heart was beating so hard I could hear it. Then I said it. I spoke the words softly. "This is Tom, dad." I said. "I just want you to know—I love you. I love you so much. Thanks for everything."

At that moment, his head moved, jerking toward me like a wind-up toy whose spring had all but run down. His eyelids fluttered, opening slightly, then closed again. The muscles in his bony face twitched and contorted, and his dry, shriveled lips did the same as they struggled to form words and speak back to me. But all that came out were some vague, distorted, unintelligible mumblings. It didn't matter though, because I knew what he was trying to say. He was trying to say, " I love you, too, Thomas. I love you, too." To me it was as if he'd spoken them loudly and clearly over the public address system at Fenway Park.

The moment lasted but a few seconds, and when it was over he returned to his motionless, comalike state never to speak or move again.

Two hours later the hospice nurse's prediction came true.

That was fifteen years ago now, and to this day I'm tremendously thankful

I finally had the courage to tell my father, on no uncertain terms, that I loved him. At the same time, I wish I'd been able to tell him long before that awful day and under a very different set of circumstances. Happier ones. Healthier ones. God knows, I'm sure I had plenty of chances over the years.

To date, my mother is still going strong, though it took many months for her to adjust to life without dad. Sadly, in the intervening years, my oldest brother Steve has passed away, too. but she still has me and Richie to look out for her.

Sadly, too, I must confess, my love for her is still shown more than spoken. I guess old habits and those many years of manly training are hard to break. But every now and then she'll say, "I love you." And I'll say, "I love you too, Ma."

Yeah, sure, I say it like my Dad used to, with all the grace of bumper cars. But at least I say it, because I know someday she won't be around anymore either, and then it will be too late.

* * *

John Hildebidle
Cambridge MA

Arrangement on the Dining Table

Artificial, of course - no cut flower or living plant
could live in an off-season vacation cottage. But, in sunlight
of earliest autumn, attractive —rusty leaves,
dried berries, arranged in a fine hand-thrown vase.
Much is claimed for the natural —organic this,
free-range that. But when you come down to it,
there's a fine beneficence in sunlit fraud.

Melanie Florence
St. George, UT 84770

Rural Friends

Late at night in my rural town
I walk the dog on silent moonlit streets,
hugged on one side by spotted hills,
released on the other by velvet green.

During the day, I scurry about
meeting and remeeting the same people.
Like ants in a colony,
our purposeful interactions
intertwine to make our cloistered town.

Now, after nine years,
I stoop over by the gravity
of constant association,
feeling henpecked like a feathered fish
trapped in a compact aquarium.

But a few compadres stand back
from this group:
"We understand," they say.
"Let's talk."

Secretly speaking out,
over coffee or yoga,
we exchange understanding,
and allow each other
to be who we are.

I appreciate these rural friends,
those caring freethinkers
who bob up in this sea
of smalltown sameness.
May they have gently stimulating lives!

Melanie Florence

Fickle Wind

Behind this glass,
I watch the winter wind
tease and tickle the earth.

Tumbleweeds play like children,
succumbing happily to be tossed.
Bouncing and rolling
across the brown and golden resting fields,
the wind is the instigator and the tumbleweeds react,
together acting as carefree partners
in ambling exploration.

But stiff grass skeletons
resist the wind's manipulation
by gripping stubbornly to the earth.
Their empty shells fall under the wind's sweeping hand,
and spring up in defiance when released.

The wind reponds with gusts of fury,
until it tears away a weaker plant remnant,
carelessly plays with it,
then thrusts it aside,
like a forgotten toy.

If Not for Spike

Melanie Florence
St. George, UT

As we waited for our foreign exchange student to arrive, the discordant clamor of voices and thumps from the nearby baggage carousel disconcerted me, not to mention the crowd pressing forward. After a week of unpacking, alone in a big house except for Keith's shy Doberman, Spike, this commotion was almost too much to bear.

But I couldn't let Keith see my apprehension; it would only increase the distance I was beginning to feel between us. Instead, I protested one last time. "Keith, I still don't feel comfortable taking in someone so soon."

"Come on, Zoe. I thought we came to an agreement about this a long time ago," Keith said, dismissing me with a shake of his head. "Having a high school student living with us would give you someone to talk to, something to do. I just don't understand why you're suddenly closing your mind like this."

I wanted to tell him that "we" didn't make this agreement. He had agreed for both of us. But I kept silent, knowing how Keith could twist my simplest of statements into an accusation.

Feeling stupid and awkward, I stared up at his profile. "Sorry. I just didn't realize how hard it was going to be to live so far away from my family and friends."

He flapped his lips in derision. "What family? What friends? Your family doesn't give a hoot about you, you know that. And your friends? Why they tried to keep us apart, remember?" Holding his fingers up to denote a quote, he mimicked in a high voice, "'Don't marry Keith. He's not trustworthy.'" Dropping his hands, he scowled down at me. "Now, what kind of friends are they?"

I bit my lip; it was true. My banking buddies had frowned upon my recent marriage to Keith. They had warned me that I was foolish to move across the country with a man I hardly knew. But I didn't listen. I had been awestruck and flattered that anyone so incredibly handsome could be interested in mousey, inferior me.

"So give me a break," he continued. "You know how much trouble I've gone through to get this organized. And besides, it's too late to back out now." He peered at me with his gorgeous aquamarine eyes, and smiled broadly. "We're going to make a fresh start once Sabina's here. You'll see."

I melted at his attention, as usual. "All right, Keith. I'll give it a try." Then, to my embarrassment, I tittered.

Ignoring my response, he nodded. "You know you need the company."

Back to reality, I nodded back. The houses were far apart in our new neighborhood, and Keith commuted to D.C., leaving me alone in our isolated home twelve, thirteen hours a day. I had only met one grizzly old neighbor who had come to our front door a few days ago after he had caught Spike chasing his chickens. Spike had run away from him, he said in a gravelly voice that matched his face, but he had followed Spike home.

"Now that I know who this damn dog belongs to," the old man said, pointing to the dog held fast by my grip on his collar, "I'm going to call the police if I catch him in my yard again." He shook his fist at me.

I looked up at his bristly chin. "Sorry, Mister . . . ?" I asked, extending my free hand.

The man didn't move an inch. "McCain. Buster McCain."

I dropped my hand. "Sorry, Mr. McCain. I had no idea Spike wandered so far away. I thought he was hanging around here. You see, we haven't built the fence yet and I hate tying the dog up."

"Humph. Just what we need around here," the man grumbled. "Another city slicker turning their dog lose in the forest. Well, I won't have it." Turning on his heels, he stalked back to his rusty pickup truck and stopped. Giving me a sour look, he said, "If I see your dog on my property again, I guarantee that you'll be hearing from me."

This memory dissipated as a new throng of arrivals poured down the walkway. Comparing faces with the blurry photo of a brunette I held in my hand, her bleached blonde hair threw me off. But I recognized that pixie face. "Sabina!" I called out, waving.

Her chocolate eyes lit up at the sight of me, but flickered when her gaze rested upon Keith. I shrugged it off. Keith's chiseled face and unusual eyes had that effect on women.

Sabina exited the pen and made a beeline toward us with a smile on her face. I felt a stab of envy. She walked like she was sure of herself, positive. Why couldn't I be that way?

"Mr. and Mrs. Johnson?" she asked tentatively in a slight Slavic accent.

"Yep, that's us," I said, smiling to cover my discomposure. Stepping forward, I gave her a hug. She withstood it with a stiff back and the skin on the back of my neck prickled. I had a feeling that Keith and Sabina were communicating a silent message over my shoulder.

Releasing Sabina, I turned to Keith and clutched his arm for reassurance. To my dismay, he stiffened below my hand and looked down at me with his eyebrows pressed down. "What now?" he asked.

I quickly removed my hand. "Oh, nothing," I said, standing up tall. Sabina didn't need to know about what a klutz I was. She didn't need to know that, in my preoccupation with her arrival, I had tripped at the top of the stairs, bounced down at least eight steps and wound up with skinned knees and a lump on my forehead from conking it on the tile landing. Keith had been right behind me, he said, but it happened too quickly for him to catch my arm.

I turned my attention to Sabina. Her resume had stated that she had taken six years of English, but that could mean anything from fluency to incomprehension. To test her, I asked, "How was your flight?"

She barely glanced at me. "Long but uneventful."

I nodded, pleased. Her accent was barely noticeable. We'll be able to understand each other from the start, I thought. That will make her adjustment to America and our household only that much easier.

I touched her arm. "You know, I almost didn't recognize you with your blonde hair."

A look of alarm flashed across her face and just as quickly disappeared. "But I thought all you Americans liked blonde hair," she said defensively.

"Oh, I didn't mean anything," I said, raising my palms. "Your hair looks great."

She looked down. "Don't worry, I'll fix it," she mumbled to her shoes.

"But you don't have to fix it," I insisted.

"Just drop it, Zoe," Keith said, grabbing my elbow. "Come on. Let's go get the bags."

We stopped at a highway diner before setting off on the long drive home. While Sabina gulped down a cheeseburger and french fries, I asked her what other foods she liked and what she disliked. I also told her what to expect from our house and small town. I concluded with, "I haven't completely unpacked yet, so you'll have to excuse the boxes everywhere."

Sabina lowered her gaze. "Oh, if this is not a good time for my stay—"

"No, the timing's great," Keith interrupted. "We decided to go ahead and take a student right away. Otherwise, we'd have had to wait a whole year."

There he goes with that "we" stuff again, I thought. But I forced myself to nod my assent. No need to put Sabina in the middle of our marital spat.

At home, Spike sniffed Sabina once and began growling with his ears down and teeth bared. I was surprised; Spike usually welcomed new people into the house. I held out the back of my hand to him, murmuring, "It's okay, Spike. That's a good boy. It's okay."

Spike sniffed my hand and bowed his head to me submissively. After I scratched him behind the ears, I turned at the sound of receding footsteps and saw Keith's hand resting on Sabina's back as they went up the stairs together.

"Zoe, go ahead and take care of Spike while I show Sabina her room," he said over his shoulder.

My heart pounded. Something felt wrong here. Even Spike had picked it up. Kneeling down, I lay my cheek upon his back. "I don't have a good feeling about her either, Spike," I mumbled into his short fur, "so you and I are going to have to stick together." I stood up. "But for now, I think it's best for you to stay outside. Now, don't go running off." I opened the front door and released the dog to a makeshift pen I had set up between the forest and our house.

Then I started making my favorite company dish: lasagna. As I was layering the pasta, cheeses and meat sauce, I heard, "Is it okay if I use the downstairs bathroom for this?"

Sabina had come up behind me without a sound. I jumped at her voice, dropping my stirring spoon on the counter. Red sauce splattered the white tile and spotted my white apron. I whirled around and saw Sabina holding up a box of a brunette hair dye.

The mess forgotten, I said, "But you don't have to change your hair color back, Sabina. You look just fine how you are."

She smiled thinly. "But Mrs. Johnson—"

"Call me Zoe," I interrupted. "Mrs. Johnson makes me feel old." I peered at her, grasping for the first time that she appeared to be much older than the seventeen-year-old high school senior she was supposed to be.

She dropped her gaze to the floor. "Okay, Zoe. You may not approve, but I want to change my hair color back."

I set my hand on her arm. "Listen Sabina. It doesn't matter whether I approve or not. It's your hair; you can do what you want with it. Let me just get you some old towels and show you the bathroom, okay?"

"Thank you," Sabina said, giving me a side hug. When she withdrew her cool arm from my side, it slithered away like a snake. I shuddered at her stroke, but covered it up by movement. "Follow me," I said, walking out of the room.

In the bathroom, I rummaged inside a box until I found a frayed towel. "Here you go," I said, handing it to her. When she took it from me, I noticed with a start that we stood evenly, eye-to-eye.

"Did you happen to get into town yet?" she asked, tossing her straw-like hair back from her face.

I answered honestly. "No, Keith's had the car. But I intend to go check it out soon."

She nodded, smiling with satisfaction. "Then we can learn the town together, right?"

I turned away to hide my uneasiness. "Where did Keith go?" I asked.

"He is upstairs in his study," she said a little too promptly.

I left her then, thinking that I needed to lay down some ground rules for Sabina, some boundaries. I also needed to talk about her strange behavior with Keith. But would he listen? That was the problem.

Sighing, I walked back into the kitchen, telling myself that I was the woman of the house; I should be able to handle Sabina. Then I wiped up the mess on my apron and the mess on the counter.

I had just put the garlic bread into the oven when my eyes caught a small movement. I spun around and had a shock. Without blonde hair, Sabina looked remarkably like me. She had my build, my height, my hairstyle. And now she had the same dark coloring.

I swallowed heavily, trying to force my fears down. "We almost look like twins," I managed to say.

She nodded. "You are quite right. We certainly do."

But as I stared at her, I could see subtle differences. Her teeth were larger; her bite was different. The bridge of her nose was longer. And, unlike mine, her earlobes were attached.

The need to talk this over with Keith became urgent. "Could you set the table for me? The plates are here, the silverware's there," I said, pointing to various cabinets and drawers. "I'll be right back."

I untied my apron and headed toward Keith's study. Pausing in the doorway, I said, "Dinner's almost ready."

Keith looked up distractedly from a pile of papers. "I'll be right down."

"But first we need to talk."

"Can't you see that I'm in the middle of something?" he snapped. "I'm sure whatever it is can wait."

"But—"

"I said I'll be right down," he said, glaring at me.

Cringing inside, I left him to his work. As I walked down the stairs, I told myself to stop agonizing over every little thing. So what if Sabina looked like me? We could turn it into an opportunity somehow, have great fun with it.

But at the dinner table, I felt tension in the air. Although Keith and Sabina sat directly across from each other, they hadn't exchanged one word or glance since I had sat down. On the other hand, they were both paying particular attention to me.

Keith poured me a glass of Merlot and then held up his beer. "Let's have a toast to new beginnings," he said cheerfully. But behind his words I sensed a falseness.

Perhaps Keith and Sabina were already having personality conflicts, I thought. Perhaps that meant Sabina would be leaving. Perhaps Keith had finally realized that it was too soon to be having a third person in our household.

Then I remembered what Keith had said yesterday; that we needed to show a united front against our exchange student from the very beginning. I nodded to myself. That's why he sounds so false, I thought. He wants to discuss this with me in private before talking to Sabina.

Under Keith's watchful gaze, I obediently clinked my glass to his beer can and Sabina's water glass, then sipped my wine. I raised my eyes to meet Keith's. He nodded to me and smiled, but his eyes didn't seem to be sparkling like they usually did.

I glanced at Sabina. In spite of the cheeseburger she had eaten only a few hours ago, she was bent over her plate, shoveling in the lasagna. She must have sensed my attention. Raising her head, she spoke with her mouth full. "This is good, Zoe."

I caught a glimpse of her red, chewedup food and felt the edges of an upset stomach. Pushing my half-drunk glass of wine away, I reached for the garlic bread.

But Keith stopped me by giving my outstretched hand a squeeze. "Drink up. This is celebration time." Releasing me, he topped off my glass and handed it to me saying, "Let's have another toast. To good times ahead."

I acknowledged his toast and sipped my wine again. Now, on top of my upset stomach, my head began to spin. I must be coming down with something, I thought, setting the glass down with a thud. Nevertheless, I needed to get tomorrow straight.

To Keith, I said, "If you let me drop you off at the train station tomorrow—" I stopped myself because my tongue felt thick in my mouth. But I had to finish my train of thought. "I can register Sabina at the high school."

Through the fog clouding my thoughts, I saw Keith shoot a troubled glance at Sabina before responding. "Oh, you don't have to worry about that, Zoe. I'll take care of it. I'm taking the day off tomorrow, remember?"

"But I thought . . . ," I pressed my lips together as thoughts swirled around my cottony brain. Had he told me he was taking the day off work? He must have.

"All righty," I said. I heard my words come out slurred, but I soldiered on. "Don't forget; we need to talk tonight."

Frowning, he threw down his napkin. "Why?"

My mind went blank. Why what? What did I just say? In the pulsating room, I pushed my chair back and tried to stand up.

"Whoa," I said, catching the back of my chair.

"Are you all right, Zoe?" Keith said, speaking in my ear.

His smooth voice pierced into my throbbing brain and reverberated inside it. I stared at him. His aquamarine eyes grew and shrank, grew and shrank and I raised my finger, intending to tell him so. But before I could utter a word, his hands gripped my upper arms.

"You must be suffering from your fall yesterday." Keith's icy voice pinged around again in my brain. "Perhaps you had a concussion."

Sabina materialized on the other side of me. Speaking in a tinny, megaphone voice over my head, she said, "Let's take her up to the guest bedroom to lie down."

The guest bedroom? I wanted to shout, but my mouth wouldn't cooperate.

Then Keith took one numb side of me and Sabina took the other. I couldn't feel a thing, but when they dragged me up the stairs, I heard my feet hitting against the steps and saw the stepsa move below me. They laid me flat on my back and tucked in the sheets around me, like a funeral shroud.

"She is not in pain, is she?" Sabina whispered.

"Shh, my darling," Keith whispered back, hovering above me with aquamarine eyes that were hard as stones.

They left me alone behind a closed door, frozen on the bed. He had called her darling, I thought with a stab of pain. He doesn't love me; he loves her. That's when I understood. Keith had chosen me because I looked like Sabina. And I had stupidly told him about my uncaring family and my very few friends. I had fit perfectly into his scheme. After he moved me across the country into an isolated house where no one would miss me and I would know no one, Sabina would replace me.

But I hadn't told Keith about Spike and the chickens and the grizzly old man. My hope rested with Spike. My head exploding, my body filled with lead, I pleaded silently, Please, Spike, please. Escape the pen and get the chickens, Spike.

Then, just before my world turned black, I heard the doorbell ring.

Lovesick Blues
By Billie Louise Jones
Hot Springs, AR

"You got to see him sing it. He does his legs in and out and he twists his hips around cranking hisself up to get that yodel out."

Buck Porter was doing his own legs in and out and swiveling his hips, there in the middle of the Timber Beast on Saturday night. Everyone looked. This thing was, his gut swung one way when his hips swung the other.

"He look like you?" Ella Jean the waitress said. "I pass."

"Naw, he's skinny as a rail."

Buck sat back down at the round table he kept for himself in the corner his establishment and tipped up his bottle of Lone Star beer to refresh himself after his exertions.

"I got this picture autographed after the show." Varina, Buck's wife, rooted around in her purse and pulled out the picture. "I want to put it on the wall behind the bar. Even if he never has actually been here."

Ella Jean held the picture thoughtfully. A white Stetson was pulled low over a face so thin it was pared down to the bare essentials of a face, just a wide, thin mouth, high cheekbones, and large, hollow eyes. His smile was a line across his face, so spare it was enigmatic, mischievous, or tragic. The signature scrawled on one shoulder: Hank Williams.

"I want to see him," Ella Jean said.

Someone put a nickel in the jukebox. The opening bars of music were instantly recognizable, even before Hank yodeled the first words; Lovesick Blues was everyone's favorite song right then.

The Timber Beast was a raw wood bar and barbecue shack just outside a lumber camp town. Behind it, almost in the woods, was a row of one room cabins for truckers and any travelers who might pull in at night. The roads through the piney woods of East Texas were narrow and dark. The Timber Beast's yellow light blazed welcome, warmth, food, drink, company.

The lumber camp workers homed in on the Timber Beast after work, like a club. Their world was dangerous. Lumberjacks blew out the tension they would never admit to feeling at the *Timber Beast*. Buck had been a jack himself before he hooked up with Varina, a bar girl who persuaded him that there was more in catering to the needs of boom town workers than in working. Once he got down out of the trees, Buck let go and never again did anything he considered to be work. Varina, with help from makeup and henna and a good girdle, held onto to what she had.

Ella Jean moved around the tables and behind the bar, planning. She could think about things even while flashing her perky waitress personality. She was seventeen. She had worked at the *Timber Beast* since she got all the school she wanted three years ago. She had bright blonde hair which dipped over one eye, high cheekbones, movie star makeup. Her pink uniform was neat; but there was something about her, not messy, not even rumpled, something that seemed like she had just got dressed, again.

She was walking past the bar when Doyle Haggard stretched out a long arm and pulled her close to him.

"I'm working," she protested and elbowed him hard in the ribs. "I got to fetch those boys another round."

"They just haul the logs," Doyle said. "They can wait while you talk to a jack."

Doyle was a real high baller—a very fast, expert, daring lumberjack. Leaning against the bar, Doyle grinned down at her arrogantly. He smelled like pine trees.

"I'll talk to you plenty after work," she whispered.

She lifted his cigarette out of his fingers, took a deep drag, and put it back in his hand.

Ella Jean carried a tray of drinks to the table of men who drove flatbed trucks of logs from the woods to the sawmill. All but one of them joked and flirted with her. Jimmy Thompson looked at her. She acted like she hardly noticed him, though of course she was well aware of every man's degree of interest in her.

Buck turned off the juke box and yelled, "Closing in ten minutes!"

Some of the patrons finished their drinks and headed out the door; others waited out the last ten minutes.

Buck pulled out his Colt and yelled, "Pay up and get out!"

He fired a round into the ceiling. That always cleared out the place.

During all this, Varina methodically counted out the cash register and Ella Jean cleaned off the tables.

Ella Jean stepped around a mess of vomit by the front door. Doyle was waiting for her by his car, a black Ford with curved bumpers. The parking lot was covered with gravel; otherwise, everything would get stuck in mud. Ella

Jean picked her way carefully. Doyle gave her a cigarette as soon as they were in the car, and she snuggled close to him.

"I want to see Hank Williams sing," she said. "Take me to Shreeport. Let's go to the *Louisiana Hayride*, stay in a hotel, eat in restaurants, buy me some clothes."

"Aw, naw, baby. You can listen to the Hayride on the radio."

She flounced across the seat next to the door. When he reached for her, she slapped his hand.

"I'll get you for that, baby," he promised, meaning that he thought taking her was taming her.

She laughed at him.

Ella Jean had slammed her bedroom door on her grampaw's hands and left home three years ago. She went to one of the towns that grew up around the logging camps. She stayed in a rooming house. Her room was small, bare, and clean. It was furnished with an iron bedstead and a chest of drawers. She had some movie magazines on the floor by the bed; but her treasures were displayed on the chest of drawers, a radio and a record player and a short stack of black .78 records in paper sleeves. She put on *Lovesick Blues*. and danced around the room.

Doyle dropped his Army duffle bag on the bed and watched her. She set the arm to play *Lovesick Blues* again and moved as if she were oblivious to Doyle. He took a record in a new sleeve out of his duffle. She saw that and danced closer, reaching out. He held it over his head. She jumped and snatched at the record. She forgot she was mad at him.

"Stop teasing me, you old meanie. Let me have it! Oh! 'Smoke, Smoke, Smoke that Cigarette' —Tex Williams. I've wanted it for so long."

While the new record played, he lit cigarettes for both of them and opened some beer. She inhaled deeply and took a long swig.

"Hey!" Doyle said. "Think you can climb this tree?"

They ate breakfast in a diner across the street. The smell of bacon, eggs, and coffee made Ella Jean smile. If Buck and Varina did not give her barbeque and french fries at work, she would often be hungry. Feeling good, she went back to wanting to see Hank Williams.

"You sure can think of ways to spend a boy's money," Doyle griped.

"What else is it for?"

She really could not understand why he would not take her to Shreveport when she wanted so much to go. After she bawled him out, and he went away mad, she really did not think about Doyle. She was too busy planning how to get to Shreveport to see Hank Williams. She had to get someone to take her.

Jimmy Thompson pulled his log truck into the *Timber Beast* for an afternoon break. The place was quiet. He watched Ella Jean. She glanced past him.

He was always hunched defensively; apologetically; and he was a sorry looking thing, face too narrow, eyes too close, skin pitted. Then she looked directly at him. No thought was necessary. She just knew what to do. She went to his table and sat down. She rested her elbows on the table, her chin on her clasped hands.

"If you're going to look at me, suppose I just sit right here and look at you?"

He turned red and tried to mutter something. He had no line at all, so she had to talk for him.

"Do you think I don't want to be friends? I've seen how you like to sit quietly and listen to the music. I love music, too. That's my favorite song on the jukebox. Why don't you take me to Shreeport? We can go to the *Louisiana Hayride*, see Hank Williams, stay in a hotel, eat in restaurants, buy me some clothes."

He understood.

The Shreveport Municipal Auditorium was a massive brick building. At least half the license plates in the crowded parking lot were from Texas. Some people drove all Friday night to go to the Hayride on Saturday. Ella Jean clung to Jimmy's arm and looked around at everything and everyone. Eyes bright, lips parted, she was excited just to be entering the place where so many wonderful things happened. She wore a new red sundress which bared her shoulders and arms; she had that look of just gotten dressed, again.

They found seats near the front, between a farm couple and a stylish city couple. She heard the farmer say, "I hope ol' Hank's sober tonight." The Auditorium was cavernous and hot, but Jimmy got them cold drinks. By then, he was easy with her pulling his pack out of his shirt pocket and getting a cigarette for herself when she wanted one.

Five minutes before eight, a tall man wearing a black cowboy outfit came out from behind the curtain.

"That's Horace Logan," the farmer said.

Ella Jean looked at Logan intently: he was on radio, "the voice of the *Hayride*."

"Welcome to the *Louisiana Hayride*." He asked, "Do we have anybody here from, hummmm, Arkansas?"

Someone yelled out, "Hot Springs!" People started yelling and naming their states. Jimmy and Ella Jean shouted, "Texas!" Logan picked out some states.. ..Louisiana, Missouri, Mississippi, on and on, while all the Texans yelled, Texas! Texas! Texas! Till they were ready to bust.

Logan said, finally, "Anybody here from.. .Texas?"

And the Texans cut loose with a roar of sound - at that moment the *Louisiana Hayride* went on the air, over all that jubilation, and the curtain went up.

All the artists who would be on that night crowded onstage in their glittering cowboy and cowgirl outfits, suits and ties, ruffled gingham dresses, prom dresses, whatever they wore, a varied crowd. They sang the theme song, while one tall, slim figure was a magnet to Ella Jean's eyes. Then everyone left the stage except the first act, a bluegrass-flavored duo called Johnnie and Jack, known for *Poison Love*; and they rode a swell of excitement from the opening. The show kept on like that, one thing after another, always changing, never stopping a moment.

Hank Williams smiled when he heard the applause as soon as he stepped onstage. He wore a brown tweed suit with dark brown Western style piping and a white Stetson. His band, the Drifting Cowboys, wore matching outfits and white hats.

"What are you going to do for the people tonight, Hank?" Logan asked from the Master of Ceremony's stand on the side of the stage.

"There's this little song I wrote after me and my wife, Miss Audrey, had the biggest ol' fight - in fact, it's the first song I ever did sing on the *Hayride*."

Hank swung into *Move It On Over*, twinkling at the audience, funny, yet singing the doghouse song at some point where hellraising met despair.

"Listen to that rascal sing!" the farmer said, slapping his overalled leg.

Calls for *Lovesick Blues* sounded over the applause. Hank grinned back at the Drifting Cowboys. Ella Jean could see the look on the band's faces when they hit the opening bar of *Lovesick Blues*, knowing the crowd would go wild. And it did. Hank's long legs went in and out and he twisted himself, getting that yodel out; and on the chorus —Hank wailing "lo-oo-ove sick blu-oo-es" — Ray Bartlett, an MC, a funny little man, jumped up and touched his toes. The crowd clamored. Ella Jean heard herself call Hank's name. The audience was like one person cheering and calling for more.

Hank edged toward the wings, knowing he would be called back for an encore. The Drifting Cowboys did not even move.

"I believe that calls for an encore," Logan said blandly. "Do you have anything else for the people, Hank?"

"This here's a song by my good friend, Leon Payne. It'll be out on record soon. I hope you folks like it."

Lost Highway. Ella Jean was so wrapped up in the star's spell that she went with him down the road from honkytonking to desolation. Her own heart swelled with misery and broke, and she cried big tears. A moment of silence; then people were on their feet applauding.

"I think you've got another hit on your hands, Hank," Logan said.

The stairs to the artists' entrance were very steep, and an off duty cop held the public back. When the artists came down, they signed autographs. Ella Jean held a picture out to Hank Williams. He signed it, and his fingers brushed hers.

She felt the touch all the way back to the hotel room, where she threw herself on Jimmy Thompson.

Now he was mooning around her all the time.

In the *Timber Beast*, Ella Jean and Varina put all the hurricane lamps out on the end of the bar, in case they lost power. It was raining bad, a cloud burst, and getting worse. The storm got so dark and heavy that they were not surprised to see the convoy of log trucks coming back. Wind and rain whipped in the door with the truckers. They went at once to the bar. Ella Jean heard them telling Buck that they turned back because there were flash floods down the road and they might have to put up for the night. Jimmy Thompson looked at Ella Jean, but she never thought about him.

Bolt after bolt of lightning streaked the sky, making it bright as day; and Ella Jean saw two Cadillacs pull off the road before it got dark again and the thunder broke.

A group of men wearing cowboy hats pulled low and carrying music cases rushed inside. All the lights went out.

Ella Jean groped her way to the end of the bar and started lighting the hurricane lamps. She had done this before. She set lamps down along the bar and carried them to tables and booths.

The men in cowboy hats were at a table near the window. Ella Jean put a hurricane lamp down. She was about to make friendly waitress remarks when she saw how the light flickered on one man's face. It caught the deep, tragic eyes and sharp cheeks; when he turned to her, she saw his smile like a line drawn across his face. She gasped.

"Are you Hank Williams? I saw you on the *Hayride*. You are my favorite artist of all time."

"I hope you keep feeling that way, honey."

He asked if they served food, and she brought barbecue and beer. She made a little extra fuss setting out his napkin and utensils. He glanced at her and said, "Why, you look like my wife, Miss Audrey, and she is the most beautiful woman God or the Devil ever made."

Even in the dim light, Ella Jean blushed with pleasure and confusion, to be noticed by him.

She could not stay away from that end of the room. Sailing by the table, she overheard enough to understand that he had tried to call Miss Audrey, but she did not answer; and now there were no phones.

"Everything will probably be back on in the morning," she said, moving in quickly. "And the creeks generally go back down about as fast as they rise up."

Drinking and talk and cards in the lamplight, while the sky shuddered and blasted. The musicians took out their instruments and strummed softly.

Ella Jean danced in circles around the tables, in and out of the light. A man's hand touched her shoulder. She knew it was him even before she turned to face him. They danced in the dark.

She went with him to one of the cabins.

Jimmy Thompson woke up with his head on a table. He had slept in a booth. The storm had slacked off overnight. The day was grey, there was a steady drizzle; but the roads might be passable for log trucks. Through the window, like a moving picture show, he watched the musicians loading their instrument cases into the Cadillacs.

There was a little girl in a pink dress, soaked to the skin, with them. She was crying the way a child cries, open-mouthed, wiping her eyes. The thin man put his arm around her and walked her off to one side. He kissed her cheek and said something to her, then got in one of the cars. They drove off. The girl watched them go, then turned.

And Jimmy saw that she was Ella Jean, without her movie star makeup, her hair wet ringlets, small and forlorn.

She ran back to one of the cabins.

Jimmy pounded one fist into the table and cursed her.

"Forget about her, hon," Varina said kindly. "Just remember the good times."

Jimmy went out to his truck. He reached into the glove compartment for his Smith and Wesson. There was a half pint bottle in there. "One swaller finishes it." He hurled the empty into the woods; and with the gun, he strode to the cabin.

The Insurance Salesman
By James Clifford
Charlestown SC

The coal cart jerked forward causing J.D. Barrings heart to skip a beat. A wave of panic seized him as he fought an almost overwhelming urge to jump out of the cart and run. God! He hated coal mines. You would have thought after more than a hundred trips down into the black pits of hell he would have been more used to it. But he wasn't, and if anything, he seemed to grow more anxious, more afraid every time he was forced to take a trip down into one of the God-forsaken holes.

The cart slowly started to pick up speed as it began its descent into the bowels of earth. "God damn brother," he cursed, knowing his chance to flee from the mine had passed.

He was the lone occupant in the cart and he took a deep breath trying to quell the panic surging through his body. Why in the hell was he doing this, he thought for maybe the millionth time. He wasn't a miner. He was an insurance salesman for Christ's sake! He had no business even being here.

His heart pounded almost uncontrollably and despite the cool dampness of the mine he began sweating profusely as the tunnel grew narrower, darker. He felt sick with the realization that money and his brother were the only reasons why he made these foolhardy trips.

After their father had passed away the two brothers had inherited his life insurance company—a profession that J.D. didn't even really care for, especially since his father, in his infinite wisdom, had given Walter fifty-one percent of the company while he controlled the other forty-nine percent. That small difference in ownership basically made him nothing more than a glorified employee so just as it was in his childhood, he was relegated to taking orders from his older brother.

The company had struggled for years until Walter came up with a sales idea that even J.D. had to admit was brilliant. The brothers began offering, for only a couple dollars per paycheck, high risk life insurance policies to coal miners. And in West Virginia, there were plenty of coal miners to buy their policies.

But it was where they conducted their life insurance sales, along with their famous slogan—"Be Wise. Be Insured" that set them apart from their competitors. They made their sales pitch in the mines because Walter believed that if they went down into the miner's territory, where they worked, it would demonstrate to the miners that they were "blue collar" guys and it would give their sales pitch more credibility. Plus, it was a known sales fact that people were more likely to buy insurance when they thought they were in harms way. And if you didn't think you were in harms way in a bottom of a coal mine—well, then you were just plain crazy. Walter's plan had worked and they were selling policies like hotcakes.

The only problem with the scheme was that J.D. was the only one who went into the mines to sell the policies. His brother came up with some lame excuse that he couldn't go into the mines because he had supposedly been diagnosed with a respiratory condition and he was under doctor's orders not to step foot into the mines. A complete bunch of baloney if you asked J.D. because the "supposed" doctor was Walter's long-time drinking buddy and he long suspected that his brother was simply too afraid to go into the mines.

The cart began descending at a steep angle and J.D clutched his safety harness for the hundredth time to make sure it was secure. He also rechecked his briefcase and bag of biscuits.

The biscuits weren't for the miners, they were for the rats. J.D. had quickly learned that rats were a miner's best friend in the world. Evidently, the filthy vermin possessed uncanny survival abilities. They could smell poisonous gases from miles away and had an almost sixth sense in detecting even the slightest movement in the earth. To a coal miner there was no greater safety device than the rodents and they not only brought the rats down into the mines but they especially made sure they were fed and well-cared for because if the rats suddenly disappeared, they had done so for a reason and that could only mean one thing—it was time to high tail it back to the surface. About the only common element in mining disasters were reports of large numbers of rats streaming out of the mines just before disaster struck.

J.D. only brought the biscuits because when a cart came down from the surface the rats would converge on it expecting to be treated to food. Some of the rats J.D. had seen were the size of small dogs and there was one rat in this particular mine that had to be a world's record. The miner's affectingly called it "Fat Boy" and J.D. swore it must have weighed close to twenty pounds.

The descent gradually became less steep and he could tell the cart was close to its final destination by the increasing loud echoes of drilling. The cart brought him around a curve into a small cavern and stopped. J.D. grabbed his briefcase with the insurance applications along with the bag of biscuits. He shook his head in disgust. In less than a minute, a dozen or so of the filthy beasts had gathered outside of his cart. They anxiously stared up at him with beady red eyes and twitching whiskers. A few even stood on their hunches with their tongues hanging out and tails wagging. They looked just like a pack of wild dogs.

"God damn brother," J.D. cursed. "Here you go you filthy beasts."

J.D. threw the biscuits into a dark corner. The rats scurried over to their food and J.D. watched with revulsion as "Fat Boy" appeared out of nowhere and began exercising his dominance by biting and muscling his way past his smaller brothers to get the lion share of the food.

He turned from the feeding rats and spotted Howard, the pit boss. He forced a smile and headed over to him. A large factor in their success rested upon the cooperation of the mine owners to gain access and convince the miners of the merits of life insurance. But that came with a price and they paid the mine owners large sums of cash for the access—a practice that was highly illegal.

"Hey Howard, how's it going?" he yelled over the noise.

Howard turned and gave him a look of astonishment. "What in the hell are you doing here? Does Weston know you're down here?"

Weston owned the mine. "Of course, didn't he tell you I was coming down today?"

"Hell no! You've got to be out of your mind coming down here?"

"What are you talking about?"

Howard grimaced. "You guys must really be desperate for business. Didn't Weston tell you?"

"Tell me what?"

"This shaft could collapse at any second."

J.D. felt his stomach began to flip. He swallowed hard trying to fight the wave of nausea rising up from his stomach into the center of his throat. "What! What are you ... Why in the hell are you here then?" J.D. stammered.

"Hazard pay. Weston's giving us three times the normal pay. There's a ton of coal deposited here and the boss wants to bring up as much of it as he can before the safety inspectors shut him down for good."

Howard laughed. "You insurance guys are unbelievable. Anything for a buck, huh? C'mon, I'll get the men. It's time for their break anyway . . . but make it fast. I don't want to be down here any longer than I have too."

To hell with his brother, J.D. thought. He was going to cut his sales presentation down to a couple of minutes, sign up one or two of the boys and then he was going to high tail it out of there. He wondered why Weston hadn't told him about the danger then realized that today was his weekly pay off—it's always about the money.

The miners gathered around him. They didn't look too happy considering the situation, but at least they were getting triple pay. All he was getting was a shortened life span due to all the stress these trips were causing.

He sped through his abbreviated presentation extolling the benefits of securing life insurance to protect one's family and concluded with their famous slogan, "Be wise. Be Insured."

The miners stared back at him with empty looks and for once, J.D. didn't care if he signed anyone up. The miners went back to work and he hastily stuffed the applications back into his briefcase.

Suddenly, one of the miners shouted, "Hey! Where did the rats go to?"

J.D. blood turned cold. He anxiously looked around—he didn't see a single rat. He stood, frozen as the miners frantically searched for any signs of the animals. After a couple of minutes Howard broke the eerie silence, "okay boys, I think it's time we head up."

"Let's get the hell out of here!" one of the miner's yelled, setting off a stampede towards the coal carts. The miners rushed past J.D. almost knocking him to the ground and in the melee his briefcase was thrown to the ground. He stooped down and began picking up the papers when Howard grabbed his arm and yanked him up. "Leave your damn papers. C'mon, we have to get out of here."

They started to run towards the carts when J.D. heard a noise straight from his worse nightmare. A low rumble gave way to a loud roar then the ground started to shake. He stopped dead in his tracks—he was so scared he couldn't even move. He felt Howard push him and then the walls began to shake so violently that J.D.'s mind refused to even comprehend what was happening. He stared in disbelief as the walls began to crumble around him.

He was thrown to the ground then the shaft was swallowed by pitch blackness, followed by a deafening silence.

"Are you all right?" He felt someone shaking his shoulder. "J.D., are you okay?"

He opened his eyes, coughed violently and saw Howard crouched over him. It took a few seconds before he fully grasped where he was and what had happened. A cave-in! But at least he was alive. He had survived.

"Yes. I think so," he managed to reply.

J.D. sat up. His clothes were covered in dirt and he was missing his right shoe. Damn, he thought. He had just bought the dang pair of shoes last week.

He looked around. They were in a tiny crawl space.

"What happened?" he asked.

"The shaft collapsed."

"Well, at least we made it," J.D. said.

Howard shook his head but didn't say anything.

"What about the others?" J.D. asked.

"Crushed to death."

J.D. sighed. "Unlucky bastards. How long do you think it will be before we're rescued?"

Howard began to laugh. "Rescued! What in the hell are you talking about! We're the 'unlucky bastards'. At least those guys are out of their misery."

"But they'll send a rescue team for us. Right?"

"You fool. No one is coming for us. The air will run out soon. We're dead men."

J.D. rolled over frantically searching the wall of rock for a way out. He quickly realized they were trapped. And then it hit him, Howard was right—they were dead men. The enormity of the situation caused J.D. to begin sobbing.

The crying surprised him, he hadn't cried since he was a kid. A rock slammed into the back of the shoulder. "Ouch!" he yelled out in pain. He turned back over and looked at Howard who had another rock in his hand.

"Why'd you hit me?"

"Because … stop crying like a big baby. At least do me a favor and die with some degree of honor."

J.D. wiped his eyes and sniffled. "I'm sorry. I was just thinking about my wife and kids. What will they do without me? How will they get along?"

"Well, at least they'll get your life insurance money. Look on the bright side. At least you can go to your maker knowing your family will be taken care of. Just like you talk about in your sales presentations."

Howard's statement caused J.D. to cry even harder.

"Jeez you're pathetic. What in the hell is wrong with you now?"

J.D. wiped his eyes with his tie. "I never took a life insurance policy out on myself."

"What!" Howard snorted. "You don't have insurance!"

J.D. nodded his head which caused Howard to break out in a fit of laughter.

"I'm glad you find this so amusing," J.D. said

Howard stared at him with a look of disgust. "You are unbelievable. You've been taking money from what little these guys make all this time—all on the premise of financially protecting their loved ones after their death. And you never bought a policy for yourself. What in the hell were you thinking about?"

"I … I never thought anything would happen to me. I never thought I would need it."

"Ya, right. You never thought you would die, eh," Howard grunted.

J.D. rolled back around and curled his body into a ball. He stared at the wall of rock facing him—it was his coffin. The oxygen dwindled and J.D.'s breathing became labored and he slipped in and out of consciousness. He knew he was close to death.

As the final wave of blackness spread though his mind, J.D. had a last thought before his mind shut down for good; "Be Wise. Be Insured."

J F Pytko
Huntington Beach, CA

Esperanto

Time plays hide and seek
with every season. Plays by its conditions
to fit its agenda that has the cleavage
of a femme fatale with a persona
that purrs with goodness and sweetness.
Time doesn't wear out like a shirt
or camisole put together by sweat
and tears for the foregone conclusion
of survival as rags in surgical buckets.

Spring is wrapped in a shroud
of peace proposals and weighted down
by leaves and branches crushed
by tank treads and uniforms tailored
by shrapnel. The remains of daffodils
are stiff as pongee sticks,
and crocuses are bent into crabshells
on the grave of the Faerie Queene.

Self possessed we move along to align our existence
with our understanding limited by the traitor of our being.

Becoming is an animal
that has a leg up on being. Is easier understood. Embraces

the bosom of the future, wraps
its arms around the overweight ego. From a burp of dust our taste
buds pop like pimples.

A shadow dance stretches arms
and legs until they break like strings.
And the heart and soul,
life's Romeo and Juliet,

J. F. Pytko

are plagued by a question
and answer duet.
And water tries to act
as if its birthright
was a well, waiting
to be uncovered by Rachel's return.
But turn the page and behind the scene
it is water from a river in Korea.
Water that licks bodies bloated upstream.
And clouds are moist like a mass
of sodden Q-tips, and a fat fog chokes
on a buoy's bell and smells
like an audience with unwashed feet.

And Summer was smoke
from burning bones and roses
that drove the locals from towns
into caves to herd like clans.
Their inherited war cries
thinned the blood of animals
and forced them into an early
hibernation. And the women
chewed on pine tar and mothered
rusting dolls.

The children on the island
of twinkling ABC's,
and plump breezes spun
from Humpty Dumpty waterfalls,
laugh as high as the highest tree,
and savor fruit as sweet
as an angel's kiss.
But not the infant in a trash bin
with a paper bag for swaddling clothes.
Never developing a facial expression,
not even for death. Dying before death
flashed its claim check to claim
a paper bag with an infant in it.
Never crying, the infant;

J. F. Pytko

never pursing its lips,
never turning on the switch
of its lips to find a light to suckle.

And autumn is heckled by birds
without wings. Birds who are bored
with songs and seeds and crumbs
of bread on toxic window sills.
Autumn's foliage is the color
of river clay oozing orange grease.
Geese and apples are pitted by vapors
from a sulfuric acid pit.
Below the pole of an invisible flag,
schoolyard children are stuck
in suspended animation.

So we breathe and eat
like professionals having degrees
in respiration and the fast food arts.
Never mind the beyond: great
or miniscule. Does it matter
if there is no substance
or magnitude? Or if mystery
is the sticky stuff in a gutter
that resists the broom
of a medium who failed to pay
its union dues to the local chapter
of the spirit world?
And the shadows reared by glaciers
prepare to slide into villages
and cities, and replace the heat
that maintains the blood's cozy temperature.
No matter its color.
No matter its electrical flow
that peddles the brain an energy
from lollipops of logic.

Winter was begging an unknown god

J. F. Pytko

to reclaim its right to be a solstice.
In their vestments of ice and snow,
the priests of winter were preaching
about salvation to be found
in freezing in the comfort
of an early demise.
The homeless men were absorbed
by the cardboard boxes they slept in.
Women wailed in streets
and tore their clothes
without ever reaching flesh.
And the night was a battle
between caryatids and gargoyles
that smashed each other
into stone confetti.

Songs enter the wind
and add acceleration to it.
But bullets do not require lyrics
to increase their velocity.
Soldiers move without songs
or a wind,
without an endorsement
of the celebrity caucus.
And a body count
is a body count.
And death doesn't need a CPA
to keep count of dead soldiers,
who are sprawled on the trash
of war:
their faces reflecting
the outrage at the loss
of light.

Joyce S. Mettelman
Naples, FL

Rash-o-Mon

My beautiful friend is dead.
Some say it's because she was beautiful;
Because she dieted away the weight that divides "matronly" from
"svelte;"
Because she re-found lost athletic strengths
And emerged from the mask of her maternity.
Because, like any newborn, she discovered the world Joyfully, openly.
When she awoke, she found herself the prisoner of an insecure,
grown-up
Little boy who would not or could not believe in himself.
Because she saw her children abused, her friends negated, her self
Exploited.
Because she tried to change it all too fast:
Trying to stay sane, get help for them both, hang on to the marriage
But couldn't.
Because, with the Gordian knot of marriage severed,
All his knots came undone.
Because a loving nature and cheerful outlook
Acted as a magnet to men and women alike;
Because, unknowingly, she had been the anchor of his fragile craft;
Because he could not reach beyond the tragedy of his life
To find himself.
Because, simply, a gun was available in any Colorado drugstore;
Because he chose the negative over the positive
Because, because, because.
For all of these
My beautiful friend is dead.

He speaks:
"She's dead, my only love.
Because she left me in the dark—
At first, busy always busy with those kids—
But I came first.
She loved me, kept my house, birthed me a beautiful child;
She cooked, cleaned, gardened and shopped,

Joyce Mettelman

Sewed her clothes and the kids'
Fucked me good and always, always loved a party or a dance.
Always looked good, tho' she got a little heavy.
But who cared? It made her look so . . . motherly.
A great hostess she could really set a table, bake
Make people feel at home.
And friends? Tons of them. . .
She even packed for me, wherever I'd go.
Always on schedule; I could count on her.
But now she's dead, my beautiful wife,
Because she got thin and sexy-looking,
Started playing tennis and skiing.
Wanted me to mix with all her friends with their "liberated" ideas.
She was just a housewife, for Christ's sake!
Just a cute kid I met then found again
When my marriage went bust and hers was on the skids.
And those kids!
Mine, hers, then one of ours —
All handsome and gorgeous, the girls too sexy
I knew they were whores—they drove me nuts.
So she's dead.
Because. . . because she wanted a divorce;
Because she got a job modeling, showed herself off to everyone.
Went to dinner with guys like a God-damn adolescent!
Dressed up in those sexy clothes from that store where she worked.
Because I followed her and saw her meeting men,
Because she took away my life.
Screamed when I hit one of her kids,
Told me I didn't have to be a hot shot to be happy.
Then flirted me into buying her something she wanted.
She wanted everything.
Dragged me to a counselor because I needed help, she said.
I could kill her!
I did.
See what a woman can do to a man?
Because I loved her so
Because I'm so alone
Because she wouldn't belong to me anymore —

Joyce Mettelman

My beautiful wife and I are dead."

Chorus:
"If she cheated on her first husband to marry him,
How could he trust her?
How could she trust him?
She was such a flirt, flaunting those huge boobs and talking innuen-
does.
Not to mention the drinking—his and hers—
And what a material person!
Clothes and jewelry, fur coats,
That huge house in the 'best' area—

She drove him to it!
He was such a sweet guy, took care of his business,
Loved his golf, skiing, his father
But she wanted everything.
So what if he didn't go to college?
But he felt he had to prove himself.
And those kids —too many, all too beautiful and spoiled.
(You know what I mean.)
Then, after the separation —the men.
Dates and parties and dinners out—
She was like a teenager running wild.
Believe me, she goaded him into it:
See what a woman can do to a man?"

In my dream, Maureen, we kneel together on smooth slate sidewalks
Where we used to skate.
He stands nearby, just looking at us.
I reach out, take his hand, shout
"I can still love you both!"
Still.
You are both still.
Years after the fact of your gun-shattered bodies
That I will never see again
I dream you alive.
Reach out to touch you, my own dear ghosts
And learn for sure that you are gone.

Joyce Mettelman

Progression

In the beginning I was ambivalent about school:
I loved the ritual of it, the familiar knowable structure.
Like the ship we built out of wooden blocks in kindergarten
Or the miracle of seeds that grew into plants in half an eggshell
On the first grade windowsill.
But I hated having to understand questions and know answers.
In second grade, some boy dared another to kiss me
At the pencil sharpener. He did, and I never forgot it,
Always afterward loved kissing and being kissed.
Did I associate it with courage? Or just admiration?
I initiated the first kiss on the first date with the man who became—
And still is—my husband. He has those greeny-hazel eyes,
You know-the kind that flash green when he wears that color.
It's a color I never wear, the only shade besides beige
That makes me feel drab and uninteresting, colorless.
Clothes do interest me; they're artful, an indication of personality,
Another form of expression. Like music: I learned to play the piano
At age nine and still collect old sheet music, trying to replace
The collection that my mother gave away when she sold
Our old player piano while I was away at college.
I never forgave her; those '40's pieces I'd bought weekly
At the 5 and 10 recorded the years of my growing-up life.
Gone—a personal record of that time and place and people.
So this progression circles back to ambivalence,
To that love/anger always present between mother and daughter.

* * *

Grace

I pass her house—bright aqua shingles on a shabby corner lot—
And I am six again,
Walking Christmas-lit streets with Grace.
Hand in hand, we scout the trees that shimmer in living room
                                                    windows,

Joyce Mettelman

Finally agreeing on the most beautiful:
One that's tall and shining with tinsel, silver balls and blue lights.
Grace changed my quiet Chanukah home—
Just candles, a brief prayer and gelt—
And gave me Christmas morning:
A stocking filled with fruit and candy, a toy piano and a doll.
She was a red-haired, freckled Irish girl, my Grace.
Later, married to silent Henry,
She grew huge with wanting child.
His dark house, with its closed-off front room
That had once been a store,
Stacked with dead boxes of toys I was not supposed to open,
Became her prison and, sometimes, my refuge.
Looking back I see that she fulfilled all those dictionary definitions of grace:
She exuded "a sense of fitness or propriety,"
She had "a disposition to be generous or helpful"
And I was "in the state of being protected."
She graced my life, gave me love and showed me another facet of the world.
Sad for her,
I was always someone else's child.

House Devil, Street Angel

By Shirley D. Kinsey
Harrisburg PA

Once upon a time there was a couple who lived together unhappily for fifty years. Her name was Alice; his was Jake.

Alice and Jake met as teenagers, married at twenty, and settled down in a two-bedroom Cape Cod in a small town in New Jersey. Alice nurtured her garden instead of the children they never had, and Jake worked at a ticket booth on the New Jersey Turnpike until he retired at the age of sixty-five.

Now, the couple always shopped together, attended church together and participated in all the more popular small-town social events. There was bingo at the Senior Citizens Center on Wednesday nights, and square dancing at the fire hall on most Saturdays during the winter months. Alice and Jake were loved by all.

"And where's Jake today?" asked Mabel Dutter as Alice was checking out at Super Fresh one Friday morning. She'd just unloaded a cart full of paper products, along with a gallon of Haagen Dazs Dutch Chocolate ice cream, Jake's current favorite. Mabel quickly scanned the rolls of paper towels and toilet tissue, and rang up the total, $26.72.

"He's at home, sleeping," replied Alice. "He still tires easily, and sleeps late most mornings." She counted out the bills from a brown leather change purse. It was worn around the edges and the clasp didn't always close tightly, causing the change to gather in the bottom of Alice's black shoulder bag. She scooped up the coins and counted out the seventy-two cents, dropping them into Mabel's hand.

"That heart attack sure did scare everyone. We wouldn't want to lose Jake. What a nice man! He'll love this Dutch chocolate. Paper or plastic, Alice?"

Alice smiled, helped Mabel fill three plastic bags and pushed her cart through the door and out onto the parking lot. It was a blistering day in August. The heat bounced off the asphalt and scorched her face as she steered the cart towards her 1989 Ford Taurus.

She dumped the bags in the back seat, turned the A/C to high and hurriedly drove home before the Haagen Dazs melted all over the already stained, gray upholstery. Alice noticed the seat was covered with dog hair again, and something that looked like mozzarella cheese. There was an empty box on the floor that had recently held a personal pan pizza.

"Jake, I'm home," she shouted, stuffing the gallon of ice cream into a cramped freezer. The icy air felt wonderful, and she reluctantly shut the door. She could feel the rivulets of sweat between her breasts, and her blouse was sticking to the small of her back. She grabbed a paper towel from the holder on the sink and swiped her forehead, and the nape of her neck.

"You look like hell, Alice," said Jake, lumbering into the kitchen in a faded pair of shorts. At one time they'd been dark green, but now they almost matched perfectly with the painted walls of the kitchen. The gray hair on his bare chest was sparse, and the vertical scar from his by-pass surgery was red and puckered. "Your blouse is all wet and your hair looks like you just got out of the shower. Can't imagine what people in town thought."

"It's ninety-four degrees out there, Jake. Everyone looks this way," she replied.

"No one ever looks as bad as you do, Alice. What did you buy? Did you get my butter pecan?"

"You asked for Dutch chocolate and that's what I got. It's in the freezer," said Alice, filling a small sprinkling can from the kitchen faucet. Friday was the day to water her inside plants.

"Dammit, woman, don't you ever listen to me? I told you six times to get me butter pecan. Well, I don't want that damn Dutch chocolate." Pushing Alice aside, he opened the door to the freezer, removed the gallon of ice cream and dumped it into a large trashcan standing at the end of the sink.

"Guess you don't have any now," said Alice. She removed the ice cream from the trash and carried it to the garbage can outside the kitchen door. It was already melting, and the sticky chocolate dripped on Alice's sandals, and seeped between her toes.

That evening Alice and Jake went to a potluck dinner at the First Presbyterian Church, where they'd been married almost fifty years before. Alice dressed in a short-sleeved, blue gingham dress and slipped into a pair of navy blue sling-back pumps. She'd decided not to wear panty hose after she'd put her finger through her last pair trying to force them over her sweaty hips. No one would notice, anyway.

Jake was waiting impatiently for her on the front porch. His wide, angular face was closely shaved and the ring of thin, gray hair encircling his head had been wetted down with a washcloth. He was a large, burly man whose body was no longer hard and muscular. The flesh of his upper arms was loose, and his muscles flaccid below the short sleeves of his sports shirt. Jake's recent cardiac problems had given his face a pale, gray pallor. He stared at Alice with faded blue eyes.

"About time you're ready," he grumbled. "Why don't you have stockings on? Any decent woman wears stockings to church."

"It's too hot, and we're not going to be in the church," replied Alice. Actually, she thought she looked nice and cool when she'd caught a glimpse of herself in the long, wood-framed mirror hanging in the downstairs hall. Alice was a short woman with sea-green eyes and auburn hair streaked with gray. Her face was a classic oval shape with a thin, rather pointed nose and a cleft in her chin. Eating the right foods all of her life had paid off. She was still thin and shapely.

"All the other women will have stockings on, and you'll look out of place, as usual," Jake said, turning the key in the ignition. "And probably nobody will like that three-bean salad you're holding. It's not one of your best."

They drove to church in silence. Except for Jake's verbal abuse, it had been fifty years of mostly silence.

The social hall was crowded when they arrived. Mabel Dutter was greeter tonight and gushed when she saw Jake and Alice. "Oh, we're so glad you're well enough to be with us tonight, Jake. How are you feeling? I know your recuperation must be frustrating for you."

Jake took Mabel's hand and kissed her on the cheek. "I feel great, Mabel, but I'll never look as wonderful as you. Alice has taken good care of me since my heart attack. I thank God every night for such a devoted wife." He patted Alice on the shoulder. Alice smiled and greeted Mabel, moving slightly out of range of Jake's hand.

"Did you get to eat that Dutch chocolate Alice bought for you today? I know it's one of your favorites."

"It was delicious, Mabel. And so refreshing on a day like today," Jake replied.

Martha Denninger and three other members of the Ladies Auxiliary rushed forward to greet Jake and Alice. Jake hugged each lady and assured them that he felt just fine.

"My, what a lovely couple. Alice is so lucky to have a man like that," Alice overheard Mabel remark to Martha as they walked away.

There was chicken pot pie, cole slaw, creamed corn, salads and apple pie for dessert. Potluck suppers were popular, and no one ever went away hungry. After the table was cleared and everyone was served coffee or tea, a beautifully decorated cake was rolled out from the kitchen on a large cart.

"Fifty years ago today Jake and Alice were married right here in this church," shouted Mabel Dutter. "Congratulations to two wonderful people!"

Alice's face turned crimson as she stepped forward to cut the cake. She hated being the center of attention. Jake thanked everyone, either shaking their hand or kissing the ladies on their cheeks.

Jake had forgotten their anniversary; Alice remembered, but didn't care.

The remainder of August was hot and humid. Alice weeded her garden and tried to keep up with a bumper crop of tomatoes. She stewed, froze and canned them, filling her freezer and stocking the wide, wooden shelves in the basement. She made jelly from the currents and grapes she picked from plants that had grown for years in the back yard. Alice froze blueberries and sour cherries, almost filling the large chest freezer in the basement. Gardening was Alice's salvation. It took her out of the house and away from Jake. She loved summer. The confinement of winter was tough.

Near the end of the month, Jake decided to take a trip to Pennsylvania to visit his nephew. Alice wasn't invited, nor did she want to be. It was three days she could relax and do as she pleased.

"I'll expect a gooseberry pie when I get back, Alice. They're ripe and ready to use. I'm taking Herbie with me," he said before he left. Herbie was the hound that lived in a doghouse on the corner of their lot. He was Jake's hunting buddy.

With a sigh of relief, Alice watched him pull out of the driveway. She immediately went to the phone and made an appointment for a facial and hair cut, and another for lunch with her friend, Janet.

"He must be gone for a while," said Janet when she heard Alice's voice. Janet was the only woman in town who was not enamored with Jake's charms. Jake didn't like Janet, and discouraged their friendship.

"Yep, until Friday," replied Alice. "I thought we could have lunch and do some shopping tomorrow."

"O.K. by me," replied Janet. "I know we've been over this before, but why don't you leave the bastard?"

"And go where and do what without any money?" Alice had never worked outside the home a day in her life. There was no social security, no retirement fund. Everything they had was in Jake's name, including the house. And she had no family.

"I told you. Move in with me."

"He'd just find me and make your life miserable, too. See you tomorrow." After Alice finished talking to Janet, she sat on the back stoop and admired her yard. She'd won first-place last year in the Garden Club's Most Beautiful Perennial Garden contest. There were hollyhocks surrounded by flocks and Sweet William. Hostas bordered the oval plot that Alice kept watered and free from weeds.

Alice had established an elaborate herb garden, which the Garden Club visited each year. She was known as the local herb expert. At the May meeting, she'd given a talk on the medicinal benefits of herbs.

She noticed that the gooseberry plants were loaded and definitely needed to be picked. Alice grabbed a basket from the garage, and headed for the end of the yard. She passed the rhubarb that had mostly gone to seed by now, but noticed that there were probably enough young, red stalks for a pie. Alice loved rhubarb pie, not one of Jake's favorites. She'd make a pie for herself while he was gone. Filling her basket with gooseberries and the rhubarb, she felt as carefree as a teenager.

Alice carefully dressed in the lilac silk blouse and black linen slacks that Janet had given her. It was her very best outfit, and she felt elegant as she rushed to meet her friend for lunch at Max's, the only four-star restaurant in town. Lunch was always Janet's treat.

Janet was waiting at their usual table. "Hey, don't you look smart!" she said, rising to give Alice a hug. They'd known each other all of their lives, and Janet had not wanted Alice to marry Jake.

"You're gorgeous, as usual, " replied Alice. Janet was tall, busty and blond, everything Alice had always wanted to be. But there was no room for envy in their relationship. Janet was much too caring and giving for Alice to ever resent anything she had or did.

"Are you enjoying your freedom, dear?" asked Janet. "No, don't answer that. I know you are. There's that glow about you that I never see any other time."

Alice laughed. "You know me so well. I worked in the garden most of yesterday and this morning, and tomorrow I'll bake pies. He's not due back until sometime Friday, or so he said. I suppose he took enough medication to last him that long."

"Maybe he'll get lost – or in an accident," said Janet. "Isn't he about due for another heart attack?"

"Janet! He's still a human being."

"Just barely. I don't know how you put up with it, Alice."

Alice just smiled and ordered French onion soup, and a Cobb salad.

Early Thursday morning she rinsed the gooseberries, measured out three cups for a pie and stuck the rest in the freezer. Besides wanting a pie when they were in season, Jake always demanded one on Christmas Eve. It was tradition that Alice bake one for Jake and another for Janet. Alice didn't care for the seedy pies, but Jake and Janet thought they were a delicacy - the only thing they had in common.

While the pie was baking, she stuffed green peppers for the freezer, cut up the rhubarb she'd collected from the garden, and prepared more blueberries and sour cherries for the freezer. She put the cut-up stalks of rhubarb in a bowl in the sink while she mixed the dough for the crust, and fitted it into a pan. Her mouth watered at the thought of the tart, juicy rhubarb.

Alice heard the sound of the garage door opener and knew Jake had come home a day early. With a sigh, she dried her hands and unlocked the kitchen door.

"Have a good trip?" she asked as Jake plopped a paper bag holding his dirty clothing down on the counter. Herbie bounded into the kitchen, his enormous paws tracking mud on the white, tile floor.

"No, I didn't, if it's any of your business. Joey was in a bad mood, and I forgot to take along enough high blood-pressure medicine for today," he grumbled. Jake slammed the kitchen door on his way out to tie Herbie to his doghouse.

Alice removed the paper bag from the counter and dropped the dirty laundry into the washer on the back porch. She added detergent, flicked the switch and went back into the kitchen. Jake was leaning over the sink, poking around the rhubarb.

"What the hell is this?" he asked. "You know I don't like rhubarb pie." He dumped the bowl of rhubarb into the sink, pushed it down the garbage disposal and turned on the switch.

Hot tears welled up into Alice's eyes. The loss of the rhubarb and the early, unexpected arrival of Jake were almost too much. But she quickly brushed the tears away with the back of her hand, and retreated to the back yard to weed her asparagus bed.

Alice had decided years before that she would never let Jake see her defeated.

Fall was Alice's favorite time of the year. She lovingly put her garden to bed, and then was kept busy with volunteer work that geared up again after a summer of heat and vacations. Alice read to patients at the local nursing home, delivered Meals on Wheels and managed a rummage sale at the church. Her life was full of activities and time spent with friends.

Jake was feeling better and resumed his job as caller for the bingo games at the Senior Citizens Center every Monday evening. He also continued to deliver books to shut-ins for the local library. The library had honored him for ten years of volunteerism at a dinner held shortly before he'd suffered his heart attack. Jake was always cheerful, giving of himself to the community. He was known to be honest and loyal. A real Boy Scout.

Just before Christmas, Alice managed to fit in lunch with Janet. Jake thought she was shopping for decorations to adorn the church social hall for a teen-age dance. And she did intend to do just that, but not until she had a lovely lunch with Janet.

"All ready for Christmas, Alice?" Janet asked. She bit into a crescent roll and wiped her lips with the pale pink linen napkin trimmed with Battenburg lace. You only got the best at Max's.

"I do have to go shopping this afternoon for decorations for the church hall. You know I don't bother much at home. Jake hates Christmas. And it isn't as if we have any little ones to buy for."

"You've missed having children and grandchildren, haven't you?" replied Janet.

"Yes. My life could certainly be fuller. But who knows how Jake would have treated them? I guess God knew what he was doing when he made Jake sterile."

"Couldn't have happened to a nicer person," said Janet, dryly.

"He wasn't always like this," said Alice.

"Yes, he was, Alice. You just never saw it. He was good looking, though. I'll give him that. Well, some day he'll get his."

Alice smiled and sipped her Earl Grey tea.

She went to K-mart after she left Janet, promising to deliver her gooseberry pie on Christmas Eve.

Alice browsed in the Holly for the Holidays Department, carefully choosing decorations teen-agers would enjoy. Even though she'd never had children of her own, she was very aware of what young people liked and didn't like. She'd been a Sunday School teacher for years, always preferring teenagers to small children. It kept her young. She chose gold and white crepe paper, and garlands with tiny gold stars interspersed with gold angels sitting on a cloud. The poinsettias looked sick, and she decided to stop at Paulie's Plant Emporium on the way home.

"Hey, Mrs. B.," called Paulie as she pulled into the parking lot. He was trimming an enormous spruce tree to the right of the entrance. He'd just finished stringing huge multicolored light bulbs.

"Glad to see you're doing a real old-fashioned tree this year, Paulie," said Alice. "All of those tiny white lights are pretty, but once in a while I like to see those nice big bulbs with just a star at the top."

"Got it right here," said Paulie, pointing to a large silver star lying on the sidewalk. "What can I do for you today? Too early to buy your tomato plants."

Alice laughed and said, "Wish it was spring, Paulie, so I could do just that. But I'd like to look at your poinsettias. I'm decorating the church hall for the teen Christmas dance."

Paulie showed her the poinsettias in his greenhouse, picked out five that had six blooms each, and said, "Here, I'll donate these. Put your money away. You're a good customer and, God knows, this is for the church. Teens, you say? Guess I'd better throw in some mistletoe, too." He put a half dozen bunches of the pretty greens with white berries into a plastic bag, wrapped up the poinsettias for traveling, and sent Alice on her way.

"Thanks for the poinsettias, Paulie. And the mistletoe. I see that they're the real thing, not with plastic berries, like I saw at K-mart. I'll make sure they use it for kissing, not eating," she joked. They'd discussed toxic plants at the last meeting of the Garden Club, and Paulie had brought samples.

"You and Jake have a Merry Christmas, Mrs. B."

Alice waved as she left the store.

By the time she reached home, it had started to snow. The heavy, white flakes were already clinging to the back steps when she opened the kitchen door. Jake was in front of the refrigerator and everything from the shelves was lying on the floor.

"What are you doing, Jake?" asked Alice, irritated that he'd made a real mess in her kitchen.

"Somebody has to put things away right. You're even too stupid to know where everything should go in the refrigerator. All the condiments should be on one shelf. You had the ketchup next to a gallon of milk." Jake straightened up, rubbing his shoulders.

"Now I have a crick in my neck. You'll have to put everything back. And make sure you do it like I told you."

"You're a pain in the neck, all right," Alice mumbled to herself as Jake headed for his recliner in the living room. She began to carefully place everything back into the refrigerator, grouping foods the way Jake thought they should be stored. No sense causing more misery so close to the holidays.

That evening, she took the two packages of gooseberries from the freezer to thaw. Alice mixed and rolled the dough for the crusts and placed it into two pie pans, making sure that the one for Janet was in the blue Delft fluted pan that belonged to her. Janet had given it to her on her birthday, filled with a deep-dish apple pie. Alice wrapped the crusts in plastic wrap, and set them aside until she was ready to use them.

She turned off the light above the sink and headed upstairs for bed. Before she reached the living room, Jake padded into the kitchen in his bare feet. He was in his undershorts, ready for bed.

"Forgot to take my blood-pressure medication at supper," he said, shaking a tablet from a large bottle on the kitchen table. He poured a glass of water from the kitchen faucet, and swallowed the pill.

"What are these pie crusts for?" he asked, nudging the one in the blue Delft fluted pan.

"That one is for Janet, and the other one is yours," Alice replied.

"This one isn't big enough," replied Jake, scooping up the crust in the one meant for him. He pushed it down the garbage disposal, and stormed out of the kitchen.

Alice sifted flour, added shortening, water and salt, rolled out the dough, and filled a ten-inch pie pan for Jake's gooseberry pie.

She fell into her bed that night, and cried herself to sleep. For the first time in fifty years she felt almost, but not quite, defeated.

Alice arose at 5:00 A. M. on Christmas Eve, determined to bake the pies without Jake's interference. She measured out the thawed and drained gooseberries, added water and cooked them for ten minutes. She added sugar, flour and salt, cooked the mixture until it thickened, and measured for two pies. Alice was short one cup.

Of course, she thought. She'd measured three cups each for two nine-inch pies. But Jake had thrown one away, and she hadn't allowed for a ten-inch pie. Alice put three cups into Janet's pie pan and set it aside.

What to do about Jake's pie? She tried to remember what she might have in the freezer to make up the volume and then, all of a sudden, she knew exactly what she would add.

While the pies were cooling, Alice rushed to the church social hall to decorate for the teen dance to be held on Christmas night. She thought the hall looked very festive, and hoped her group would have a fun holiday affair.

She and Jake dropped Janet's pie off at her apartment on the way to church that evening, Jake grumbling all the way that they'd be late. The candlelight service was lovely, definitely Alice's favorite. On the way home from church, Jake was quiet, and Alice was thankful. It was a crystal clear night, and the full moon cast shadows across the three inches of snow that had fallen the day before. Alice felt that all was well with the world.

"I'll take a piece of that pie, now, Alice," he said as soon as he pulled the Taurus into the garage.

Alice took off her worn, cloth coat and removed the pie from the refrigerator. She sprinkled a bit of sugar on the top crust. Jake had a sweet tooth and liked his pies heavy on the sugar. She served him on his lounge chair in front of the TV. He was watching *It's a Wonderful Life.*

"Good pie, Alice," he said, the first compliment she'd received from him in fifty years.

The ambulance arrived at the house about 2:00 AM, immediately after Alice had called Dr. Kruger, Jake's internist.

"Sorry, Alice," said Dr. Kruger, his stethoscope on Jake's chest. "I'm afraid he's gone. He's suffered a massive heart attack. There were no guarantees, you know. His by-pass didn't go well, and we were afraid of complications."

Alice brushed the tears from her cheeks, and held the kitchen door open for the ambulance crew. She sat on Jake's lounge chair as they loaded his body onto a stretcher, and then stood in the doorway until the ambulance and Dr. Kruger left. It had begun to snow again, and she watched the flakes in the beams of the headlights until the ambulance was out of sight.

Alice grabbed Jakes's old leather jacket from the porch, clutching it around the shoulders of her bathrobe while she called Janet.

"He's gone, Janet," she said.

"Who's gone?" asked Janet.

"Jake. He died."

There was a moment of silence on the other end. "How did it happen, dear?"

"He was sitting on his lounge chair eating gooseberry pie, and about an hour later he complained of indigestion and chest pain, and he couldn't catch his breath. A half hour after that, he was dead," replied Alice.

"Well, it wasn't the gooseberry pie. Mine was wonderful," said Janet.

Alice smiled and said, "Glad you liked it."

Janet sighed. "I really am sorry, Alice. But maybe now you can begin to live."

But Alice knew that life is no fairy tale, and that there are very few happily-ever-afters.

The Harmon Funeral Home was packed for Jake's viewing. It had suddenly turned warm, and the snow was mushy and gray on the streets and sidewalks. A line of mourners snaked from the wide, circular porch of the funeral home and down Main Street, past Dairy Queen. Some folks thought it was unfortunate that Dairy Queen was closed for the winter. Good ole' Jake would have liked them all to stand in line sustained by a Blizzard or Dilly Bar.

Alice sat quietly in front of Jake's casket, hands folded in her lap. She greeted the steady stream of friends expressing their sympathy on the death of such a wonderful man. One of the last to kiss her on the cheek was Matty Graham, a member of the teenage group from church.

"So sorry, Mrs. B. Please let me know if I can help." Matty's voice shook with compassion. "By the way, our dance was wonderful. You did a great job on the decorations. Just a suggestion, though. We could have used some mistletoe."

Alice smiled and said, "Maybe next year, dear."

William Beyer
Belvidere IL

The Drowning

On this summer afternoon
you enter the vast,
moving table
of ocean
from a deserted beach;
your private place.

Ignoring advance
of dusk,
possible danger,
you move out,
far beyond point
of safety,
linger a long moment,
before sudden descent
into the colder,
deeper depths;
disappear.

Indefinite ocean shadows
lengthen;
darken.

Night advances,
suggests a mood
of immediate grief;
tragedy
within the perfect sea silence.

William Beyer

The Distance; Evening

In a deserted, park,
under high roof
of gathered night trees,
I turn away
from your dark glance,
suggesting an end of love,
want to question
why it happened,
when,
but I remember
how you dislike questions;
that curious way
you habitually seek
the safety
of silence.

Between us,
in mood of midnight,
there is an extended moment of distance,
necessary caution,
and not a word
to properly express
regret that lingers
in the uneasy shadows.

The Guide
JD Baker
Rockville, MD

The sunset was finally over, and the deepening purple of twilight captured the remains of orange sky with a quick and sinuous darkening. The symbolism was not lost on him.

William Abiaka Powell briefly considered stubbing out the cigarette, then dismissed the idea with a snort. The doctors were saying it was lymphatic now, so why stop doing one of the few things left he still enjoyed? Out of sheer stubbornness he used the still-glowing butt to light a fresh one, pausing only to tear the filter off the new cigarette. Now that was it.

But the stinging pleasure of the harsh tobacco smoke was fleeting. A shooting pain in his gut doubled him over and he coughed hard into a crumpled handkerchief. He was no longer surprised to find blood spotting the white linen. He looked at the red seeping into the cloth and inexplicably thought of his own bloody heritage.

Will was named after the two greatest heroes of his Seminole people, the mightiest of all chiefs and the most powerful of all shamans. William Powell and the shaman Abiaka had fought the expansion of the white man for 20 bloody years in the swamps of South Florida, killing over 1,500 bluecoat soldiers and costing the US government over 20 million dollars before they were finally captured and executed.

His name had always seemed ironic to him, for he had never felt particularly heroic. Sure, there was the time he had been guiding a group of researchers through the 'Glades and they had been attacked by a rabid cougar. He had taken it down with his 12-gauge only after catching a raking blow from its claws. But that had been all instinct and he had shaken badly after. A discreet pull from his hipflask had quieted his trembling hands while the aghast researchers tended to his wounds so he could take them back to Chokoloskee. No, he was no hero. But he was a guide, and a damn good one. Truth be told (with a bit of hubris) he considered himself "The Guide."

From the time he was old enough to drive an airboat, he had been in the 'Glades. When he wasn't acting as a guide for tourists, government researchers, climatologists, local police or search parties, he was wandering there on his own. The spray from the giant fan of the airboat would spread, misting behind him as he sat with one weathered hand grasping the tiller and another clutching a cigarette. It was his life, and he loved it. It was his own way of staying true to the roots of his people and honoring his ancestors.

He hadn't been out since he'd been diagnosed a year before, following a spate of stomach pains that wouldn't go away. He just didn't have the same heart for it anymore.

That was about to change.

He snuffed the last cigarette of the day and headed inside for bed.

It was not an easy sleep, for the pain that wracked him was the worst at night. The pain medication had long ago stopped working, so he long ago stopped taking it. But finally he drifted away. And he dreamed.

He was 12 again and sitting on the dock behind his old family home near West Lake, a cane pole in his sun-browned hands. Of course, Grandpa Powell sat beside him, sipping coarse black coffee in companionable silence.

But as he looked up at his grandfather, he realized with a start it wasn't him at all. The man beside him was ancient, wizened in years far beyond the 60 which had been allotted to his own grandfather. This man was as old as the earth, dressed in the traditional robes of a tribal shaman, and he looked down at young Will with bright eyes. In spite of his aged appearance he projected strength and authority, and Will realized that this man was as to his own dear grandfather like a shooting star is to a firefly. In spite of those smiling eyes Will was afraid.

Then the ancient spoke, and he no longer feared.

* * *

Will awoke with every detail, every word as fresh on waking as it had been in dreaming. It had been no ordinary dream. His Grandpa Powell had told him stories of Dream Visits that would come to chosen members of the tribe, but he had never really believed the tales. He believed them now.

Will sped all the way to Chokoloskee, his old Ford pickup topping 90 as he chain-smoked.

His airboat was still tied to the dock. Tyler, his nephew, had been maintaining the boat on odd weekends. Will had planned to leave the boat to the boy.

Instinct took over, and it was just like old times. The engine kicked over on the first try and the fan sped up until it became a blinding, blurry circle. He eased into the chair (like he never left it), and gripped the throttle with a strength he hadn't thought he still possessed. He opened the choke and the airboat moved out from the dock. He took care to stub out his cigarette in the old coffee can by his feet and shook his pack. Only one more left.

Will knew every swamp, every lake, every stream and every bog in the Everglades. He sometimes felt he knew every tree by sight as well. But guided by the remembrance (and instructions) from his dream, he quickly found himself traveling impossibly unfamiliar ways. The swamp grew thicker around him. The air seemed closer, the trees denser, the entire world more teeming with life. Alligators sunned themselves lazily on muddy banks, and wood storks fished on graceful legs. A great blue heron took to wing as he passed. He traveled in this way for uncounted hours; the water and green of his beloved world surrounded him and for the first time in a year, the pain in his guts subsided to nearly nothing.

Eventually he came to an open and still body of water, too small to be called a proper lake. In the middle of it rose a small hump of land, covered in thick grasses and hanging cypress trees. He cut the engine and the airboat seemed to glide naturally to a stop at the waterline. Directly ahead of him an overgrown trail led away from the water. He disembarked as a sense of anticipation built in him. He didn't bother mooring the boat.

As he climbed the trail, he caught a glimpse of something in the underbrush. He stumbled to a stop when he realized what he was seeing. Slowly, he crept from the path for a closer look. He suddenly had trouble swallowing, and the pain inside him returned with a vengeance. Skeletons. Dozens of them, some clad in the rusted armor of the conquistadors, some in ragged Union blues. Here and there among the weeds he spied a sword, a pike, an ancient musket, a newer Springfield rifle. Ancient battles had been fought here. Will took it all in, his mind racing. He felt unclean among the dead and returned quickly to the path.

Brushing a hanging frond out of his eyes, he reached the summit and came to a clearing. A small stone structure (temple) stood at its center, and before it stood Will's Visitor. He was the ancient shaman of the Seminoles and Will's own ancestor. Abiaka raised his hand in greeting.

Will walked before him silently, but smiling in pure joy. After years of wandering the 'Glades, he had found what he never knew he was looking for. He had come Home.

Abiaka spoke, his voice deep, grave and smiling all at once. "Hello, my boy. Come inside and have a drink."

Will followed him into the cool shadows of the temple. A wafting sense of life came from a circular hole in the stone floor. Reflected dancing light flickered around the inside of the temple and Will saw the rippling water filling the hole. Will wondered at it: good clean water, where only brackish swamp should have been.

He knew what this place was.

Abiaka removed a small tin cup, battered with age, from a shelf on the wall. Engraved on the cup were the crossed swords of the US cavalry.

Will took it reverently and knelt before the well. He dipped the cup into the water and brought it to his lips. He swallowed and it hit him like a warm electric current, racing quickly through his body, curling him over his knees. He couldn't move for a moment, but when he finally was able to unclench and stand, he realized he was truly without pain. He knew the cancer was gone. He felt energized. He felt strong. He had never been so alive.

He turned to Abiaka, full of questions. Before he could open his mouth, the old man spoke for the second time.

"You belong here now, William. It is my time to depart this place. By drinking, you have become the Guardian of the Well of Living Waters. The spirits here are strong, but sometimes the unworthy stumble upon this place. It is your duty now to keep this most sacred of places hidden from an unready world."

Will thought of the dead lining the path and shuddered. Other thoughts were tumbling crazily through his mind, and he voiced the first one that manifested clearly.

"This must be for our people!" Will protested, thinking of all the wondrous things the Well could provide for the Seminole nation. Finally, a true payment for their years of suffering! A miracle that would at last bring his people out of poverty…

Abiaka cut him off with a sharp wave of his hand.

"No, William. The Well is for all people of this world. But the world is not ready for the Well. You will guard this place until the time comes when you must pass the guardianship to one of your heirs. And they will likewise serve the spirits of the Well. But someday William, the world will be ready. One of our people will come to the world and the world will receive him, and he will lead them to the Water."

Will had more questions, but Abiaka again cut him off.

"Drink again, William, and again, until all your questions have been answered," he said, tapping his temple with a long and browned finger, and continued.

"The Well, dear boy, is not of this world," he said with a smile.

Then he turned and walked down the path, disappearing into the green. Will watched him go then went back into the stone temple. He knelt before the hole, watching the light dance on the water. He watched for a long time.

Lou Bertha Collins
Andrews SC

Steal Away from the Storm

The sea was roaring
Paradise Island suddenly was no more
The pain, the cold, and the rain rustled inside my mind,
And while I lay confused in time, the visions came. . .
This is my season to love
   A strange feeling beckoned me,
   I didn't want to heed my calling
I was running for my life. . .
I couldn't look back, I didn't look back,
   Didn't look beside me to see
Someone else is in the storm tonight
I heard a long, deep cry, crying out, My Lord! My Lord!
Someone else is in the storm tonight
I reached out and grabbed her hand. . .
   We didn't look beyond us to see,
We couldn't look back, we didn't look back
We were running for our lives. . .
   I realized the earth was moving and we were falling
   A Heavenly Light shined all around us
This is my reason to love
And while I lay reclused in time, the healing came. . .
The pain, the cold, and the rain rustled inside my mind
Paradise Island suddenly was no more
The sea was silent
The storm was over.

Pat Huber
Alhambra, CA

Requiem

My love is dead.
The deep pit stomach feeling that I'll never survive.
How can I live without my soul man?
The one who hears my alien thoughts, understands the climb for
freedom.

Strange as I throw his ashes into the ocean.
A sea lion barks.
"I'm alive," Paddy says.
"I love you always."

Surprising as I find he's not dead at all,
Only in another dimension.
Love never dies,
It only changes energy form.

He's the ghost winking, playing at my bedside.
In the straightness of my shoulders as I walk taller.
Sending his leprechauns to play and trip me.
But I never get hurt.

I hear him whispering, "Grab a hold of this old ball of mud,
Go for the top and expect it.
Remember to keep you mouth shut, your bowels open,
And never volunteer for anything."

You were a rebel, babe.
Bowing to no man.
Believing in God and yourself.
A warm, loving God desiring only our good.

Thank you, Paddy.
The pain of your loss took me on a journey.
Hearing the whisper of the still, small voice
Promises of wonder, joy, love.

Pat Huber

When I felt alone nd tired
God sent you to remind me that love caresses me once more.
I hear you, darling.
I feel your kiss.

* * *

John Hildebidle
Cambridge MA

Auto Visions

For whatever reason, I skipped those usual male daydreams:
setting points and plugs, popping a clutch.
But when my mother, just as I turned into a High School senior,
chose a snappy blue Ford convertible,
I was in some vestibule of Heaven.

My dad stubbornly favored jobs that offered roomy company
                                                         cars,
New Yorkers or Coupe de Villes, to accommodate his girth.
I'd have given anything for one of those
station wagons with fake wood side panels.
It was never in the cards —those were cars people
drove to go fishing or spend a month camping.

Our summer vacations were going from customer
to customer, with my salesman dad. At least, on the road
there was air. When we'd come up behind
a wagon on some highway, the majesty of it stunned me
kids facing backwards in the rear seat, smirking,
gesturing, waving. I could well imagine the glory
of watching the world recede, making even Nebraska imperial.

The Fate of Vladi Hunyadi
by Nora J. Hamilton
New York

Although its glowing orange tip nearly reached his fingers, Emiglio Farragamo took a last courageous suck on the self-rolled cigarette. After a wheezing exhalation, he tossed what remained into a standing ashtray and broke the silence with a click of his tongue.

"Such a savage method!" he shouted. "And you, Hunyadi, with all that training as a Dentist."

Even the Brooklyn accent was eerily monotone in Farragamo's lipless slash of a mouth. Hunyadi stared despondently into the haze while the detective rolled and lit up another cigarette. Farragamo tilted his head backward and, drawing the slash into a taut circle, puffed heavily, creating a ring of smoke. The suspect pointed meekly at the dissipating ring, and even made a nod of admiration in the hope of distracting Farragamo. But the detective's uncompromising back eyes remained fixed on his as though by a magnet.

"Detective," Hunyadi began with a thick Hungarian accent, "I can assure you, I would never have done such a thing! I mean, a stake! Revolting! Do you really believe that a man of my..." he broke off when the slash formed an ironic curve.

"A man of your what, Mr. Hunyadi?"

"It's unthinkable!"

Hunyadi made an effort to square his sloping shoulders. "Good God! Running somebody through with a stake! Unthinkable!"

Farragamo grimaced, opening the slash and revealing a zigzag of smoke-stained teeth. Despite his horror at the gray and brown spectacle, Hunyadi swallowed his ever-ready repertoire of professional advice.

"My being of Hungarian descent..."

"Parents" Farragamo broke in, still grimacing dingily.

"certainly does not mean that I'm the bloodthirsty savage who, ..."

"Who, who!" echoed the detective. "You, Hunyadi, drove a stake through Claudio Da Silva! You spitted Da Silva!"

The suspect drew a crumpled handkerchief out of a trouser pocket and daubed the moisture from his face and neck.

"I did nothing of the sort" he protested in low, trembling voice. "I did noth... and anyway Mr. Da Silva was not spitted, I mean, from one end to another like a roast."

"What?" Farragamo's yellowish hue deepened.

"He wasn't spitted longitudinally like a roast! The stake" Hunyadi persisted, tucking away his handkerchief, "was driven through the man's chest, through the poor devil's chest!"

Farragamo, who had perched on the window sill, hopped onto his feet and signaled with a wave of his knobby, yellow hand to someone behind Hunyadi. A uniformed boy appeared next to the chair on which the suspect sat. In his hands was a stack of papers. The detective indicated that he should give the stack to Hunyadi.

"Read Officer Boasi's report, you skewing madman!"

Hunyadi got to his feet and pointed toward the door. Farragamo scanned him contemptuously from head to foot.

"That's right, Mr. Hunyadi, outside."

* * *

On the twenty fifth of August, shortly before 10:00 PM, the thirty year-old manufacturer of paper towel and cup dispensers, Claudio Da Silva, was murdered in his apartment. Da Silva had been run through below the chest with a wooden stake and left to wrestle with fate.

According to Senior Officer Sal Boasi's report, Mikhail and Tanya Krovoy, who lived in the apartment below Da Silva's, heard, "strained breathing and a number of masculine groans" from their neighbor's apartment at around ten o'clock. Because of Mr. Da Silva's regular weekend entertaining, the couple found nothing strange about the sounds and didn't think to investigate. But some five minutes after what they had assumed was, "the concluding groan", a loud thud, followed by the sound of rushing feet, made them suspicious.

Tanya Krovoy had begged her "curious Mik" not to do a vigilante number and even tried to restrain him. After taking nearly a quarter of an hour to convince her that there was nothing to fear, Krovoy finally, "wriggled free from the frantic girl and sneaked up the stairs to Da Silva's floor". Finding the apartment door ajar, Krovoy peeked in to see, "a tall, slender man with yellow hair bent over Da Silva's twitching body, which appeared, like a slab of marble in a dark inky pool". Out of the victim's abdomen protruded the blunt end of a rough, unvarnished stake. Krovoy slipped back down to his apartment and rang the police. Sal Boasi arrived at fifteen minutes after eleven to find the man described by Krovoy pacing back and forth next to Da Silva's cadaver. He introduced himself as, "Vladimir Tibor Hunyadi from across the courtyard". Hunyadi explained that he had been on his balcony and saw through the large living room window that the victim tumbled backward through the air with a stake in his chest. The suspect claimed to know nothing of the whereabouts of Da Silva's linen, which had been stripped from the open sofa-bed.

Boasi waited at the scene of the crime with a photographer and a coroner for the arrival of Detective Emiglio Farragamo. Two assisting officers brought Vladimir Hunyadi to the police station.

* * *

Vladimir, or Vladi, Hunyadi saw himself as confirmation of the claim that no one can escape his or her fate. In researching his lineage, the retired Dentist managed to bore his way back to fifteenth century Hungary and a warrior named Steven Hunyadi. It was no inspiration to Vladi that the Magyar was a brave sort, who, for the sake of territorial expansion, took on even the cruelest of enemies.

In Vladi's perception, his ancestor's only serious flinch was in the face of one Vlad Dracul the Second, a reputedly bloodthirsty anti-Hungarian rebel. Because of a fondness for wooden stakes and his method of impaling adversaries, the same Dracul earned the nickname, *Tepes*, meaning, "stake," and went down in history as, "Vlad the Impaler". In any case, Steven Hunyadi was one of many, who, in galloping through the rebel-wracked territory later to be called, "Romania", suddenly found himself in a forest of impaled cadavers.

It wasn't disappointment over Hunyadi's initial turn-around-and-gallop-back-out maneuver that made Vladi bring his research to an abrupt end, but the sudden and inexplicable conviction that he himself was fated to make a similar grisly encounter. The unnerved ex-Dentist not only stopped researching, but devoted all of his energy to smothering the memory of his newly acquired knowledge. When asked why he had suddenly begun to drink, Vladimir Hunyadi was always prepared with the safely mundane excuse that his marriage to Hildegaard Detlevsen was, "falling apart at the seams". The twenty year difference in age, once a sensitive point with Vladi, proved to be blessing in that it made the falling-apart-at-the-seams bit plausible. But when he took to drinking nonstop, the lie became a truth.

* * *

Once she had packed up everything of value, including Vladi's red Fiat, a broken-hearted Hildegaard left to return to her mother. In spite of her bawling and stomping insistence that Vladimir's unquenchable thirst for Kadarka, a sultry Hungarian wine, had, "driven the wedge into their marriage", Hunyadi was convinced that all the talk of warriors and stakes in connection with his heritage had frightened Hildi away. He recalled her pallor and the deep violet half-moons which had formed under her eyes when he made a sketch of his royal relative, lost among the dangling dead. But Hildi, who could never admit to being frightened, had sworn that Vladi's use of her red Dior lip pencil for the rendering of wounds had been, "the virtual last straw".

Vladi regretted his heavy handedness and, even wrapped in the vapor of Kadarka, was inconsolable. But on the second to last weekend before Hildegaard's thundering departure, light appeared at the end of the tunnel. The light poured out of a large window across the courtyard from his back balcony. Prepared with a bottle of the beloved beverage, an opera glass and a foam-stuffed kitchen chair, Hunyadi took to indulging himself on Friday and Saturday nights in a ritual of observation.

Aside from two unexercised buttocks and the callused soles of two feet, Vladi saw nothing of the neighbor, whose name he later learned was Claudio Da Silva. Flanking the adipose humps bilaterally were two slim, smooth-shaven female legs, which always strove for the ceiling. Vladi never put down the opera glass until the cleaved, undulating mass had made its last and most decisive rise and fall, and the tender, unpolished female toes had given in to the force of gravity.

Vladi Hunyadi became convinced that the opera glass constituted his key to fulfillment. But after three months of gleeful weekends, the Kadarka-slurping, voyeuristic self-indulgence came to a violent end. The most peculiar aspect of the fateful Saturday evening in question wasn't that Da Silva's rendezvous began at a quarter after nine instead of eleven thirty. Nor was it the unusually soft light emanating from the rectangular window. Not even the plumpish legs, ending in red lacquered toenails impelled Vladi to cross the courtyard and brave entry into his neighbor's apartment.

It was after the host's patrician rump had collapsed once and for all that the otherwise gratifying weekend theater suddenly turned absurd. Vladi perched in puzzled irritation on the edge of the foam-stuffed chair and waited for the extinguishing of the light, but the strangely tame glow persisted. Just as he had hauled himself to his feet with the help of the wrought iron balcony railing, a sudden bizarre undulation of Da Silva's mass drew his attention back to the window. He peered greedily into the opera glass to make his first encounter with his neighbor's upper half, and saw that Da Silva was raised up onto his knees, a jagged point protruding out of a dark, oozing rip in his back.

Although an icy lump had formed in Vladi's stomach and bitter saliva flooded his mouth, he perceived it as a good neighbor's duty to investigate. Forcing back the fluid with heavy gulps and pressing his sweat-soaked handkerchief to his lips, he made his staggering way across the courtyard.

* * *

When Vladi's case came to trial, the first witness, Hildegaard Detlevsen-Hunyadi, explained that, after her six-week recovery in Albany, she had suddenly begun to imagine Vladi tumbling about the apartment in blind inebriation. Panic had taken hold of her at the thought of him, left to himself with matches, cigarette lighters and a set of stainless steel cutlery. Despite her mother's teary protest, she had been determined to reassure herself that poor Vladi was still among the living, and returned to Brooklyn.

She had arrived on the twenty-fourth of August and, in order not to re-emerge too suddenly into his existence, reserved a room at the Morning Star Hotel. Not knowing what to say to Vladi after so many long weeks, she had hesitated before finally trying to reach him on the evening of August twenty-fifth. Given what she called his, "nearly permanent state of intoxication", it had amazed the witness to find that he wasn't at home. But close to midnight, Detective Farragamo had got in touch with her from the police station. According to Farragamo, Vladimir had rung her mother from the jail and learned of her whereabouts at the Hotel.

To Vladi's horrified amazement, Hildegaard Detlevsen betrayed his confidence, bringing every entrusted secret, as well as the contents of his diary, which she had "unintentionally" stuffed into her suitcase, before the court. The defendant even found himself confronted with the Dior-embellished battle scenes, and a highly emotional account of his, "lip-licking enthusiasm over the finished renderings".

Following Tanya and Mikhail Krovoy, Dolores Detlevsen was called to the stand as a character witness. As though her daughter's testimony wouldn't have been enough to secure Vladi behind the thick, flat prison bars forever, mother Detlevsen shoveled salt into an open wound by narrating from the, "ghastly story of the poor girls marriage." In what Vladi thought to be a strangely blissful tone, Detlevsen concluded her slanderous monologue with a reference to Hildi's, "white-lipped and trembling state" as she, "leafed through the frightful wretch's diary."

Vladi's throat twisted itself into a knot when the triumphant prosecutor informed his Honor through the ill-fitting dentures that there were, "no further questions". Only the defendant's amazement over Emiglio Farragamo's sudden appearance kept him from bursting into sobs. After a nod from Farragamo, Vladi's attorney, Rudolf Stieglitz, approached the stand in order to question Mrs. Detlevsen. The witness studied the pink, hairless man with an expression of disdain and answered his gently put questions with loud self-satisfaction.

\>>Of course Hildegaard had taken the Fiat. It was her only means of escape from that Dionysian Beelzebub Vladimir Hunyadi!<< —she begged his Honor's pardon— >>And, would it not have been criminally irresponsible to leave a motorized vehicle in the hands of one given to such a habit?<<

\>>Had Hildegaard Detlevsen taken luggage with her to Brooklyn?<<

\>>Clearly she had taken luggage!<<

\>>What kind of luggage?<<

\>>What difference could it possibly make what kind of luggage? But, if

Mr. Stieglitz insisted, a large yellow suitcase with a blue handle.<<

>>A plain yellow suitcase with a blue handle?<<

>>A yellow suitcase with a blue handle and a round New York University Decal! Was Mr. Stieglitz satisfied?<<

Vladi felt his heart sinking when a half smile formed on his Honor's massive, vain-decorated face, but the rosy Stieglitz continued in a steady voice.

>>Had Mrs. Detlevsen-Hunyadi been nervous before leaving for Brooklyn?<<

>>Whatever did Mr. Stieglitz think?<< Detlevsen's ironic tone became sarcastic, >>Wouldn't the good man himself have been edgy, having to face Vladimir Hunyadi's revolting drunkenness?<< —once again the lady begged his Honor's pardon—, >>Of course she had been nervous! Poor Hildegaard had smoked nonstop!<<

>>What type of cigarettes?<<

Mother Detlevsen couldn't refrain from giggling.

>>As Mr. Stieglitz wished. Palomino.<<

The witness' triumphant confidence as she left the stand made rage well up inside of Vladi. A stinging bolt went through him when she passed in the aisle, scanning his face with a smile on her thin lips, and his struggle against the urge to tear out the tinted brassy hair caused his teeth to chatter.

When Stieglitz requested that Mrs. Detlevsen-Hunyadi take the stand for a second time, it surprised Vladi that Hildegaard's expression wasn't one of self-satisfaction. She glared at the attorney as she ascended into the witnesses' box, and her small Dior mouth was taut. Stieglitz turned to face the courtroom entrance and made a sweeping gesture toward himself with his hand. Within a few seconds, two court officers appeared, each carrying an opaque plastic sack. Tilting his head respectfully, the rosy attorney requested that the officer nearest him present the first item to the witness. Vladi's scalp prickled when he noticed that the man wore surgical gloves. The officer reached into the sack and drew out a transparent plastic pouch containing a white bundle. When he raised the sack for presentation to the witness, a dark red blotch became visible. Hildegaard Detlevsen-Hunyadi, who had taken notice of the blotch, drew together her shoulders and clasped her head between her hands.

>>What had she to do with such a dreadful mess? Did Mr. Stieglitz find himself amusing?<<

Stieglitz' rosy face remained expressionless. He signaled for the accompanying officer to approach the stand. In the second sack was a large rectangular object. Stieglitz took hold of the bottom seam and pulled while the officer braced the object between his arms. The attorney then pointed out with agonizing gentleness that the very suitcase described by the witness' mother had been found in an ally two blocks from the residence of Vladimir Tibor Hunyadi.

Inside of the blood-soaked bed sheet, which had been stuffed into the suitcase, were three cigarette stubs bearing the brand name, *Palomino*. Furthermore, the stubs bore finger and red lip prints.

Hildeagaard Detlevsen cried out.

>>It could only be a trick of Vladimir Hunyadi's!<<

All at once a peculiar haze filled Vladi's eyes, and Hildi's frantic voice rang out of a direction which he could no longer determine. He wrapped his sweat-soaked fingers around the curved, polished edge of the bench in front of him. The rushing sound which had begun in his ears quickly reached such intensity that even high-pitched Hildi became inaudible. The white haze thickened and a searing pressure in his back was Vladi's only remaining connection to the physical world.

The end had come and, to his sheer amazement, Vladi discovered that there was existence after death. He opened his eyes to find himself lying supine with a circle of bewildered faces studying him from above. At his feet stood Emiglio Farragamo. The expression of satisfaction, almost jollity, shaping the otherwise fierce eyes irritated Vladi to the extent that, despite his post-transitional state, the muscles in his limbs began to twitch. He even felt himself balling his hands to fists. Before long, he raised the same fists above his face and studied them in fascination.

Farragamo bent forward, tearing open his lower face to reveal the familiar dingy grimace.

"It was nothing to go tumbling down over, Hunyadi!" he sniggered. "So damned squeamish! And all that training as a Dentist!"

The icy knot in Vladi's stomach as he beheld the gray and brown zigzag convinced him that he hadn't stepped beyond the boundaries of tangibility, but was very much alive. Farragamo explained through a ring of smoke that, after his, "cowardly, white-lipped retreat from consciousness, and removal from the courtroom", Hildegard Detlevsen-Hunyadi had been sentenced to, "a very long visit in prison for her grisly deed".

Vladi's eyes welled over with gratitude and, moved by a feeling akin to fraternal affection, the retired Dentist humbly offered, at no charge whatsoever, to turn Detective Farragamo's, "one and only flaw into a dazzling smile".

Diana Festa
New York,

The Offering

The Himalayas' purple sun after
the long night,
creeping from behind the mountain
suddenly over earth and sky,
one does not forget
nor birth,
the child so helpless crossing to life,
naked and bloody already,
the whimpers one does not forget
waking at night, the love, landscape
of tears and laughter, moments that turn
into space.

I searched the future in almanacs,
the geometric patterns of fear
in my room with the alarmed telephone,
two in the morning,
Carlo in the Mexican prison.
Who ever heard of Tepic, a place with flat houses,
snake lines of mothers being searched
at the jail's entrance, nakedness on naked floor
in Ouicholi land, peyote in flower pots,
the unforgiving heat, garlic in the air,
and the children helpless
in unstable architecture, circles and coils.

What can be done,
I must stop being terrified,
must be there, give my son the slice of purple sun
I saved.

Her Solo

Carolyn Scott
Birmingham, AL

Mrs. Hunnicutt gathered up her fulsome skirts and tiptoed across the dirt path behind the hen house. She rustled the clumps of grass along the branch with her heavy wooden walking stick, and whenever she found a guinea's nest buried in the bank, she tapped the eggs, then flipped them toward the water. The water seeped into the cracks she had made, and each egg drowned rather quickly. Two large turkeys gobbled from the other end of the wooden structure where they had come to watch her. She put her finger to her lips and said "Shh-hhhhh," to the curious pair. Then she went around the hen house and back to the front of her house and sniffed the wisteria she had planted there on the lattice work. "Simply divine," she said aloud with more than perfect diction. She climbed the four steps slowly onto the outside porch and finished her lemonade. She lit a vaporous candle to discourage any harmful insects that might pursue her. As she drank the last sip from her tall, frosty glass, she noticed the same pair of turkeys eyeing her from the bottom steps. "Don't you dare come up here," she said, stamping her foot. They waddled off toward the guineas who were drinking from the branch, unmindful of the terrible fate of their progeny. The turkeys gobbled, and the guineas belled back.

All the chickens, turkeys, geese and guineas were supposed to have moved with their owner, but no, the territorial fools liked her place and kept coming back to their old haunts to leave their droppings. She waved a broom at them as she went into the old board and batten house she had converted into a country manor. She filled it with her lifetime collection of art, music, books, antiques and dhurrie rugs. It was home now. She went to the refrigerator and got out the tutti frutti ice cream. She dared not put this indulgence on her list for the weight loss doctor. No. This was a little secret she would share only with her tabby, who was watching her from the dining room window. "Don't tell, Kitty Little, " she said with a laugh and dropped a teaspoon of ice cream into the cat's bowl.

The phone rang with an off-key clanging sound. Typical country communication. Why they didn't even have cable out here yet. "My dear," said a cultivated voice. "We're going to be out your way in a little while. May we drop by?"

She instantly recognized the minister's cultured tones. "Why certainly, I'm home today. Do drop in." She hurried to the kitchen cabinets and found a tin of biscotti. Then she squeezed lemons and made a fresh pitcher of lemonade with cherries floating in it. She got out the silver holders for the tall glasses she preferred, unwrapped slices of the crisp biscotti from their cellophane wrappers and soon had everything ready to carry to the parlor on a tray. What on earth did he want from her?

She snatched up the scattered newspapers and tucked her copy of *Jesus the Man* away behind her easy chair. She agreed with the authors that Jesus was the best man who every lived, and his ethic unequalled, but thought he possibly was a mortal like the rest of us. Teaching at a Christian college as she did made that an unmentionable fact in her repertoire of politics, history, medieval plays, Shakespeare, speeches of the day, and all the other subjects so dear to her heart. Her vast library of books on all sides of the den attested to the knowledge she shared with their authors.

The sudden whir of a lawn mower coming to life out back drew her to the back door. She held it ajar and waved frantically at the man riding it. "Lincoln, Lincoln," she called to his back. He ignored her and began making a pass around the cluster of fig trees. As he came around the last one, she gingerly made her way down the back steps and forced her arthritic knees to move toward him. She stood in his path, noting with dismay that she was almost as wide in shadow as the swath he had made. When she didn't remove herself from his path, the driver stopped and stared at her, mopping his chocolate face.

"Lincoln, we can't do this just now. I have guests arriving any minute."

"But Ma'am, I can't see myself getting back out here for four or five more days."

"Well, just drag those tree limbs that fell over behind the barn and weed beneath the tea roses. It looks terribly overgrown from here."

"And the cuttin?"

"When they leave, Lincoln, you can cut to your heart's content."

"If my ride ain't come."

"Maybe your ride could get you here on the weekends, if need be."

"Don't know 'bout that," he said.

The gravel roiled as the sleek black Lincoln pulled into her driveway. It was incredible that their small church had had the good fortune to attract such an elegant man of the cloth. He had retired from one of the big churches in the city and moved out to their little burg with the idea of a peaceful dole of retirement checks and few clerical duties. Now he was completely caught up in seeing their little congregation grow. This son of the old sod just hadn't known his destiny when he left the big city with all the socially elite. She mopped her brow, climbed back up the steps and hurried through the house to the front door. She noticed the minister's slender, stiff back as he opened the car door for his wife, and sighed audibly.

Mrs. McDonald was reed thin and once had been a New York model, but now she wore the kitziest clothes. Today, it was a pink denim with narrow straps over what appeared to Mrs. Hunnicutt to be a plain white tee shirt. She had on horn-rimmed sun glasses and her hands were empty of a pocket book, handkerchief or anything.

"Well, well, come in, you two," Mrs. Hunnicutt called, laughing jovially.

"Love your place," the wife said sweeping her arm in the direction of the flowers.

"Is that your creek?" the minister asked.

"Yes, I won't run out of water, will I?"

"Whose idea was this lovely trellis?" asked the wife.

"I thought of that pergola." Mrs. Hunnicutt said.

"Splendid, splendid!"

After they had their tea and biscotti and chatted about all her art and antiques, the minister asked rather abruptly about the number of beds she had.

Mrs. Hunnicutt pursed her lips before answering. "Well, I have my bed, of course, and a guest bedroom with twin beds. Why? Did you two want to come for a weekend?" She laughed again.

"No, my dear Estelle. It has come to my attention that there will be two exchange students at the high school next year, and Mr. Balfour is looking for someone of the highest character and esthetic sensibilities to host them."

"Don't they usually stay with families? With other children?"

"I thought so too," said the wife. "That could be true, but these students are coming from France, and I heard you had once studied at the Sorbonne."

"Oh, ages ago, I was there briefly. Very briefly."

"I was certain that it appeared in your academic credentials when you asked me for a reference some time back."

"I can't remember," she said, looking at the dark oak beams in her white living room. The color of the wood was just what she had wanted. "What age are these children?"

"They're nearly twenty, and from their papers, I judge quite cosmopolitan. They are both girls. You would be such a wonderful one for them to converse with."

"I'm flattered that you think so, but...." She felt herself blush.

"And your musical interests might lead them right to our little choir," said the wife.

"I've been meaning to suggest some more lofty venue for our choir. Most of what we sing was done fifty years ago by the Baptists."

"Oh, really?" The woman's neck seemed to grow longer. She was the minister of music.

"I remember singing those Baptist tunes well. I was one."

"Where is your church letter?" asked the minister. "You haven't actually become one of us, have you?"

"Well, I'm there every Sunday. I sing. I feel like I've become one of you."

"Of course, of course, we see you, we hear you, but we don't own you as our own yet," said the wife, admiring her French manicure with exaggerated white tips.

"I'm not exactly ownable. I've my own beliefs, of course, but they're not the same as...."

"Oh poppy cock," said the minister. "Let's not argue over technicalities. Jesus is the Lord of all."

"Do let me freshen your lemonade," said Mrs. Hunnicutt retiring to the kitchen where she took a deep breath and grabbed a napkin to mop her brow. She got out extra lemons from the refrigerator and quickly mixed another pitcher.

"Here we are, here we are," she sang as she re-entered the parlor.

"You make this biscotti? It's delicious," said the blonde wife with the outdated page boy style hairdo, as she crunched delicately.

"No, no. I bought this, but I have made it in the past."

"Utterly delicious and refreshing," said the minister. "So kind of you to prepare this little treat."

"So, where were you two heading when you came this way?"

"We've some business at the Courthouse," said the wife, glancing over at her husband, who looked so dapper in his white shirt and perfectly creased seersucker pants. In church, he was always hidden beneath a robe, but even then his blue eyes with their little twinkle and his thick grey hair made him an impressive figure —one the older ladies admired.

She cleared her throat. "I've health problems you don't know of, so it behooves me to ask my doctor whether a year caring for two teenagers would be the wisest thing for me."

"Well I always say," said the wife, "a grain of sand makes a pearl."

"Or it kills the oyster," said Mrs. Hunnicutt.

"You've never had children at all, have you?" asked the minister.

"No. Female problems kept me from it."

"But you were married?"

"Yes, to a professor of Middle English."

"Chaucer and all?" asked the minister.

"Whan that Aprille with its showers soote, the drought of March hath perced to the roote," she replied with a chuckle.

"Oh I remember memorizing that in high school," said the wife with a wide smile.

"Now they have it translated into modern English for the little darlings; can you imagine that?"

"Certainly not," said the minister who probably wished she had quoted Burns.

"About those hymns," said the wife. "Is there a special one that you yourself could sing?"

Ave Maria has always been a favorite of mine. She didn't add that she thoroughly doubted the virgin birth.

"That's a bit Roman," said the wife.

"Have you another favorite, Dear?" asked the minister leaning forward.

"*The Lord's Prayer.*"

"*The Lord's Prayer* would be perfect for Sunday week, don't you think, John?" asked the wife.

"Without a doubt, Alice," he said, as he sized up Mrs. Hunnicutt.

Suddenly she heard herself babbling on about being in the Glee Club in high school and staying afterward to practice with the student teacher who was in his twenties, and then practically skipping all the way home to face an interrogation by her mother for being late. Then being denied the right to sing in the choir afterward and her mother reporting the young man to the principal. When she got through she grabbed a napkin and blotted her mouth, then each eye.

"And I bet they had you scheduled to give a solo at some point," said the wife with an elbow to her husband.

Mrs. Hunnicutt nodded. She hadn't the foggiest notion whether that was true.

The minister stood up and took her hand. "Well, my dear, your hour has come. "We'll be lisnin at you, as they say 'round heah."

She laughed at his little witticism and stood to bid them adieu. After they left, she twirled around the parlor twice and sang the first few bars of her intended solo. The Malott arrangement was her personal favorite. "Our Father, who arrrrrt in heaven, Hal-low-ed be Thy name." She pronounced each syllable as if it were the most precious jewel in the world.

The sudden whir of the riding lawn mower caught her attention as a shadow fell over one of the front windows. "Oh, Good," she thought. Lincoln was back on his noisy red horse.

During the next two weeks, she began to pine for a piano to accompany herself. A couple she knew was selling a small walnut grand, and she had been longing for one for some time. She would have to cash in a CD to get the money, but fiddle-faddle. You only solo once.

She also rushed around to fabric stores getting enough voile in a floral hue to have herself a new dress made. A small voice reminded that she would be wearing a choir robe during her performance, but she brushed it aside. It was after the service out in the church yard where she wanted to look nice. She asked her dressmaker to please drop everything and get busy on her new frock. The wiry little gray-haired woman looked up from her workroom strewn with fabric scraps and nodded.

"That bitch beats all," she heard the woman tell her Chihuahua as she let herself out the door. But with all the business she had given the seamstress, she knew it would be ready.

She spent an hour a day at her new piano playing for herself and practicing. Birds outside sometimes joined her as she trilled a few bars. "Forgive us out debts as we forgive our debtors." She wondered if the French girls enjoyed singing around the piano, but then crossed that out of her mind. They were not going to stay here. It would be impossible for her to cook and feed them for a year. The costs would be extraordinary since she was something of a gourmet.

Saturday before the Sunday she was to sing, she had her hair done, got a manicure and picked up the new dress. She was trying it on when the phone squawked.

"My dear, how are you?" asked the delightfully cultured voice.

"I couldn't be better," she trilled back.

"And your decision?"

"Oh, I plan to sing, I've practically moved heaven and earth to get ready."

"Wonderful. And what about the French girls?"

She suspected a little arm twisting, so she said. "Must I give you my answer this very afternoon? I'm in such a stew getting ready and practicing my solo, and my doctor's appointment is not until next week."

"Well so be it. We'll see you in church then a wee bit early tomorrow."

"I'll be there, johnny on the spot," she said with a lilt. If she had the care of two girl children she couldn't jump up and go places any time she felt the urge. On the other hand, she wouldn't always be coming home to an empty house. The next morning, before slipping into her new dress, she added to the color of her rouge a bit and put a theatrical red dot in the corner of her eye. When she got the dress on, the button right at the waist came loose, and she had to scurry around finding a needle and thread to fix it. The cat sat on the dresser watching her. She had been jumping from table top to chair back to bed to dresser all day. Mrs. Hunnicutt's neighbor had told her this behavior was due to fleas on the floor and in the rugs. "I'll powder you the minute I get home, Kitty Little. Can't afford to get that powder down my throat until after my solo." Our Father, who art in heaven, she intoned rather majestically. Then she called the cat and got it to go out the back door. Drat, that Lincoln had left a ladder propped against the house where he had been cleaning gutters, but that didn't matter, she was going down the front steps to her car. She flipped the dead bolt on the back door and put the key above the door frame. Then she gathered her purse and white gloves and went out the front.

As she stepped onto the porch, she heard a turkey gobble. Then several other turkeys waddled up. By the time she got ready to step down the four short steps, a semi-circle of the gray vultures had gathered. She didn't know there were so many of them. "Shoo," she said, taking the first step. The rooster gobbled as they ascended the steps three abreast. "Amscray, scram, skeedaddle," she said.

The hens clucked in low tones as if plotting their next move. Not one of them would budge. She took off her hat and fanned the air with it. The porch ceiling fan immediately sent her hair flying in all directions. She waved her purse which hung from her wrist by a short gold chain. One of them grabbed the chain and sent the beaded white purse sailing into the yard, contents askew. She kicked at the closest bird, and it pecked her foot. Suddenly two flew overhead and landed behind her. She shuddered, thinking of that Hitchcock movie. "Help," she called, absolutely certain that nobody was in hearing distance. She backed up one step, but the two birds there opened their feathers and clucked out a challenge. She mopped her brow with one lovely voile sleeve. Then she checked her watch and noted there was only fifteen minutes until church services started. It took her at least twelve to drive there. She stomped one foot and there was a rustling of feathers, but no mass exodus. Where were they? the neighbors who owned this avian guerilla squad. "Help, help, help," she screamed, stomping one foot and then the other like a little girl having a tantrum. She remembered doing that when her little sister had lost her Shirley Temple doll years ago. She did it again and stepped on a bony wing, then took a tumble right into the feathery horde. They softened her fall, but she split her stockings right at the knee and the hem of her lovely new dress was ringed with bird detritus. Her ankle felt as if it were sprained. She tried to stand up, but the pain was too great. "You'll be on somebody's table this Thanksgiving if I have my way," she promised. The turkeys stood in a ring gobbling softly as if they hadn't really meant to cause this much distress. She leaned back and looked around her. All was beautiful and peaceful. Her roses, her majestic ferns, her day lilies of yellow and orange—all soothed her feelings with their lush beauty. The dogwood in the side yard with its pink blooms bowed in the soft spring breeze. "Our Father, who art in heaven," she sang, "hallowed be thy name. Thy kingdom come, thy will be done, on earth as it is in heaven. Give us this day, our daily bread, and forgive us our debts as we forgive our debtors...."

With this the brood elongated their necks momentarily, then began to back away from her slowly pecking at insects and worms and other things that interested them. Mrs. Hunnicutt continued the prayer, singing in her best form until every bird had backed off and the guineas could be seen and heard only faintly over by the copse of woods. "And lead us not into temptation, but deliver us from evil." There was nobody within earshot. She could lie here for a week. Maybe French girls in the back bedroom was not such a bad idea. She heard a power mower come to life and felt some hope of rescue. The bellows of an organ would not have been more welcome.

Mrs. Hunnicutt filled her contralto lungs for the final powerful lines: "For thine is the kingdom, and the power, and the glory, for ever and ever." Amen. She lay back against the velvety grass and contemplated the perfect blue dome of sky, her solo done.

Valerie Casses
Johnstown PA

The Elevator

It was a small room
Smaller than it should have been
Or needed to be
There was no reason
No really good reason
For the smallness
Too many people
Jammed aboard
Crowded intimately
Around him
Violating his personal space
As he unwillingly violated theirs
His breath choked
A timid rage swelled
He thought he might swoon
A hairsbreadth
Separated his valuable being
From them

And then suddenly
Like a balloon released
The tension left
Peaceful calm warmed him
Smoothed his anxious features
He stopped fretting
Stopped sweating
Stopped being so self-conscious
And smiled at the tiny woman
Burrowing into his armpit
He wrapped his free arm around
The ancient man cuddled
Beneath his chin
And backed firmly
Against the soft rolls
Of the stout matron behind

Valerie Cases

The gigantic man
Squeezing in on the next floor
Stooped
Grinning
Chuckling
And encircled them all
In his corded tattooed arms

One moment
Between floors
Breathing with one set of lungs
One jubilant heart beating
One brain rejoicing
The human beings
Filling that small space
With wordless wonder
Ascending through space
Winging aloft together

Someone stroked his leg
Not at all suggestively
But as if in friendship
As if in acceptance and love
He gathered their flesh to him
Their warmth
With gratitude
Breathed in
The shared humanity
And sighed with happiness

It was a real shame when
The doors slid open
At his floor
And he was ejected
He dragged himself
Most reluctantly away
To see his dentist
Who touched nothing intimately

Valerie Cases

With warmth and caring
Especially his rotted teath

Of course the journey down was different
The teenage girl scowled her ears plugged with shrill music
The businessman was lost involved in mental calculations
The young mother murmured anxiously to her whining childen
And he was defeated by red hot pain
Defened by pain
Unable to hear or be healed by
The Muzac in the elevator.

The Unwanted Girl
Richard Vaughn
Mission Viejo, CA

The treachery of remembrance always comes back with an insistent knock on Gram's front door frame that summer dusk in 1944 when I was eleven. Outside the screen Mr. Olafson's bulk blocked my view of the elm-and-oak-lined street. He wore faded overalls with a red plaid shirt, straw hat in hand as he gazed at her. She was in her blue cotton dress. I stood barefoot in jeans and T-shirt. Though his coming to the house startled me, I sensed the purpose. My belly growled with its cargo of meat loaf, green beans and boiled potatoes. Something had happened, and I tensed.

"Howdy, Mizzus Kuhnemann," Mr. Olafson groused.

"How dee doo, Lars," she said. "Come along inside."

"Got no time. Wonder if'n Robby iz about?"

"Uh huh," I said, since he saw me plain enough.

"What is it?" Gram asked, her voice strained.

"Reckon Robby's seen the girl anywheres."

She glanced at me, then asked him, "Bryna?"

Mr. Olafson nodded, his rawhide face stolid.

"Ain't seen her today," I said with a gulp.

"Not a'tall?" Mr. Olafson stared hard.

"No, sir. Not for a bunch of days."

Gram said, "What's going on?"

"Warn't home last night or all t'day," Mr. Olafson said, gnarled hands coiling the straw hat brim as if to crush it. "Might be she run off."

"That's mighty odd." Gram said. "Whatever for?"

Mr. Olafson shrugged. "Don't rightly know."

"Where could she have gone, Lars?"

"Don't know that neither," he said, stepping back and pushing the hat on his head. "Well, if'n you folks get sight of her. . ."

"Yes, surely," Gram said. "Won't you come in for --"

Mr. Olafson had already backed across the porch to ease down the front steps, wiping his face with a green bandana. He trudged into the encroaching night.

Gram studied me, a curious, thoughtful look that I still remember after half a century, along with her concluding, "Guess maybe it's not so queer after all."

I sort of recall Bryna's appearance, but in tiny fragments, leaving holes as if a picture puzzle with pieces lost where you need them most. She wasn't pretty like a movie star, even if she desired to be one. Her hair tumbled in shades of spring wheat, strands twisted together. Churned butter skin gave her a usual Nordic complexion for Arbordale on the Minnesota plain by Beck Lake. Her narrow forehead and wide cheek bones, however, created an exotic squint, accented by piercing hazel eyes.

She lived with her uncle and aunt about a half mile down the road from Gram's place on the edge of town. Their small one-level house looked well cared-for in the way of the Scandinavian farmers who'd homesteaded the territory. The Olafsons, Lars and Trude, had always lived there. This was my first visit to Gram's while Mom worked in St. Paul, so everything felt new. Bryna was my age, but seemed so much more mature. Same height, but she stood square and walked in her ankle-high shoes like a man.

How and why she came to be living with Lars and Trude I'm not sure because she never talked about her circumstances. Since my mother had been twice-married and struggled during the Great Depression, I figured Bryna's situation was like mine. That didn't keep me from falling in love when I first laid eyes on her.

Beck Lake had an acidic, wind-whipped ice essence even in summer, but with inlets where the water lay smooth and warm enough to swim without shivering. Not knowing any of the local boys, I explored by myself, found a secluded spot, stripped bare, and waded in. Crouching behind thick cattails I caught a splash and saw matted ropes of hair floating on the surface. Head and muscled shoulders emerged. She wiped her face with large hands, gazed at me without fear, then rose up and surged my way. The water fell below her waist and I faced a husky girl.

"Who are you?" I said. "Get away from me!"

'No," she said. "What're ya doing here?"

"This's my place, I found it first."

"Cattail Cove's only fer girls!"

"Who says so?" She scared me. "Anyhow?"

She stood right in front of me. So much girl flesh in the sunlight and shade of breeze-rustled willows and poplars made me flush. I wanted to cover my nakedness, but she seemed unconcerned. I waited as defiant as I dared even though she had first rights because she was a local and knew about things. She glared, folding her arms.

"Ya live around here?" she said, less angry while looking me over.

"With my grandmother. Just for the summer. Mrs. Kuhnemann."

"The widow lady, right? Gray slate house, weed vacant lot next door?"

"Yes." Under her gaze I felt thin and weak. "My home's in St. Paul."

"Well, this swimming hole's fer girls," she said, easing back a bit. I felt bolder and got smart-alecky. "Any girls come I'll get out."

"Oh, yeah?" She started wading towards me. "Is that so?"

"Yes, that's so," I said, but began retreating to the shore.

She slapped the water. That flung a stinging splash toward me. Some of it got in both eyes. By the time I'd wiped them she'd half-turned away again, so I splashed back. That went on for a while until she got the better of it and I quit. She waded out farther into the inlet, swam until she reached wind-rippled waves before returning. I wouldn't have tried that, having already decided there was no way to match her in stamina. By then I'd dried off with my T-shirt behind scrub bushes. After I pulled on my jeans and headed barefoot through the grass to the dirt road, she loped alongside in overalls with a sleeveless plaid shirt. Not sure what to expect, I kept walking. I felt uneasy because I'd seen the back of her thighs as she'd waded away —purple with whip-lashed welts.

It was the strangest time. We walked quiet till we came to the mailbox that I'd passed going to the lake. A dirt road led up to the farm house perched on the slope a hundred feet away. She clasped my arm and pulled me along the rutted road, wheat and barley lush on both sides. That's how I came to be at Olafson's place. Big maples shaded the house up close, and behind were scores of fruit trees —apple, peach, and apricot. The languid air flowed rich with the scent of their blooms and nectar. Some fruit had ripened and dropped onto the black earth to languish swarmed by bees and flies. The sweet odor made me dizzy. She sat me on plank steps, went inside the back porch screen door, and came out with two Kern's jelly glasses of lemonade.

Since she didn't talk, I played the game. She drank in silence with a some-times look my way, but most often glanced through the orchard as if watching for someone. Thirsty as I was, but feeling awkward near her, I sipped my drink slow. I found it tough to be easy around other people. She seemed to like my sitting beside her. Every time I felt an urge to speak, fill the hush with words, I held back. Later I heard voices from the orchard. Her uncle and aunt, Mr. and Mrs. Olafson, clumped toward us, each lugging a basket of pears. They saw us, stopped for a moment, then came right up.

"Where'd ya take yarself, girl?" Mr. Olafson demanded.

She looked at him, lips pinched tight. "Swimming."

"Shouldna done that," Mrs. Olafson said, putting down the basket to wipe her face, neck and arms with a blue bandana. "Lotsa work t'be done."

"Girl, ya know there's no time fer idling," Mr. Olafson said.

The girl shrugged. My lemonade glass remained half full, but I started gulping it down, figuring to be out of there quick as I could because I sensed trouble. She nudged my arm and winked ever so slightly that I reddened, wondering what I'd gotten myself into. She made me feel a part of what might happen next. I got even more anxious than when we first met at the lake.

"Ya know what happens, Bryna," Mr. Olafson said, placing his basket of pears on the ground. He didn't trouble to wipe sweat from his leathery face that was creased like rain-gullied soil. "When ya up and go off and such."

Before the girl could say anything, Mrs. Olafson began gazing at me as if she'd just noticed my presence. She looked me over like somebody fixing to buy livestock, examined the girl, then eyed Mr. Olafson with a twist of her thin mouth. Her face had crinkles like her husband's, but fuzzed as the skin of a ripe peach. When she spoke her words came out sugar polite, the way a person talks with company, high-pitched and extra-polite, making me more uncomfortable.

"Bryna, honey," she said to the girl, "who's yar friend?"

"Just my friend is all." The girl passed me another wink.

"I'm Robby," I said to Mrs. Olafson rather than the man.

Mr. Olafson squinted at me. "Ya from around here, boy?"

"Now, Lars," Mrs. Olafson said with care. "Manners."

He said, "Got a right t'know who she brings here."

I explained quick about visiting my grandmother.

"Ya, sure," Mrs. Olafson said, "Ida Kuhnemann. We know her, Lars. She's on Stocker Street. Puts up rhubarb and watermelon pickles."

Mr. Olafson didn't seem to care about that, staring at the girl, hands twitching as if about to grab her. But he didn't, catching his wife's eye and pulling out a handkerchief to wipe himself about the face and neck. I gave the glass to the girl, got up, and started off away from them around the corner of the house. Mrs. Olafson called goodbye. The girl caught up with me. She gripped my upper arm with strong fingers.

"Thanks for sticking a while," she said, breathless.

"Oh, that's okay. I liked the lemonade swell."

"It'll go better for me with ya being here."

"What do you mean?"

"Nothing. Bye, Robby."

"Okay, sure. Bryna." When I said her name she gave me a broad smile before returning to the house. "Goodbye." My parting word lingered in the humid air.

That night I told Gram about Bryna. And the Olafsons. She said they worked hard and raised good fruit, but were thought strange by most folks and seldom dealt with anybody in Arbordale beyond necessaries. She didn't know much about Bryna, who'd come to live with them winter '42. I couldn't help thinking about her, went to the lake afternoons hoping to meet again. Gram teased me about puppy love.

The embarrassment of that diagnosis didn't stop me from dawdling past the Olafsons whenever I could. One Saturday morning two weeks after, I saw them drive to town in their black Ford pickup. I ventured toward the house, knocked on the front door, then the back, and called Bryna's name. She ambled from the barley field like an emerging shadow, red kerchief on her head, a far away face as if half asleep. I felt she might as easily lose herself back in the field. Both hands on her hips, she waited for me to say something. I mumbled nonsense that made no impression because she looked back toward the orchard. She had chores to do.

"Can I help?" I said, longing to hang around.

"What do ya know about harvesting fruit?"

"Not a thing. Can't you show me how?"

"Ya don't seem hardy enough fer it."

That made me puff. "I am, though."

She pinched my biceps. It hurt, but I didn't flinch.

"Well, come along. Let's have a go at what ya can do."

She led me into the orchard. Bryna'd been working on a peach tree with an unpainted wood ladder against it. She showed me ripe fruit: reddish, not green. As I studied the tree and fingered several peaches, each appeared the same. She plucked a ripe peach and held it next to one unripe so I'd see the difference. After that she went up the ladder while I worked below, sneaking peeks at her while I did my best to pluck only ripe peaches. She came down, checked the bushel basket at my feet, clucked like a teacher at my ignorance as she tossed a few unripe fruit into the orchard, then climbed back up the ladder. After an hour I was hot and feared I'd pass out. She took me to the porch, threw water in my face out of a pail, then fixed gooseberry jam sandwiches on knife-sliced white bread. We sat on the steps munching.

"How long does this harvesting take?" I asked.

"Whole summer," Bryna said. "Seems forever."

"Why don't they hire folks to help the picking?"

"Not their way. We have to do it entire ourselves."

I couldn't help noticing a purplish bruise on her left upper arm. She rubbed it some, saw me watching, and stopped. It reminded me of the bruises on the back of both thighs. I must've looked somber because she grinned and patted my shoulder. It felt so special I shivered despite the warm midday. There was hardly any breeze, and the air lay moist on my exposed arms like a damp rag. Moths and butterflies fluttered through wavy space. I liked Bryna more than anybody I'd ever met, a queer sensation because till then I'd never paid much mind to girls my age. Sitting close to her left me short of breath. I felt sure we were friends and could talk about what bothered me.

"Does your uncle hurt you often?" I ventured.

"Not really much," she said, soft as a whisper.

"When you're bad, do something wrong?"

"Never bad. It's just kind of what I am."

"How could that cause you trouble?"

"When I'm forgetful, wander off."

"Why do you do that anyway?"

"Need to be myself, that's all."

"If you get beat, why go?"

She eyed me. "Secret."

That sounded so sophisticated to my childhood self that I must have stared at her like an idiot. She smiled and patted my shoulder after brushing bread crumbs from her hand and sipping lemonade for a few minutes. When she got over being inside herself and staring through the trees, she laughed.

"Robby, ya want to know what I actually like?"

It startled me, the mood shift, but I said, "Sure."

She hurried inside, the screen door slamming behind her, and rushed back in a few minutes with three magazines. They were about the movies and filled with photos. She flipped dog-eared pages so fast I couldn't keep track of what she said. Her voice got deeper as she enunciated each word with such care that it sounded as though she spoke from a stage and wanted everyone to hear. She loved Barbara Stanwyk, also Veronica Lake, but most wanted to be like Rita Hayworth. She posed when she said each movie star's name. What she talked about, dreamed about, began to seem more real than the fruit trees. I became miserable listening, wishing her life might be better somehow.

"Maybe one day," she said, putting the magazines inside the screen door.

I heard the pickup on the road long before noticing the dust it raised. We both ran into the orchard. The plan was, she told me to say that I'd wanted to help and that's why I came by. The truck groaned behind the house and braked. Bryna climbed back up her ladder and we resumed peach picking. Mr. and Mrs. Olafson strode out to the orchard moments later to confront us.

"Back from the shopping?" Bryna said from atop the ladder.

"Get yarself down here right quick!" Mr. Olafson ordered.

"What's the matter?" she said, her voice quavering.

"Ya know right enough, girl," he said, louder.

Bryna came down slow, the canvas bag almost filled with peaches. Before she could remove the shoulder strap over her head, Mr. Olafson grasped her by one arm and yanked her toward the house. She strained to free herself from the strap, which caught on one elbow, spilling peaches on the ground. They scattered like flung balls amid the dandelions. Mr. Olafson paid no mind to her distress, or me. She dropped the bag as he jerkied her along off balance.

Mrs. Olafson and I watched until he and Bryna were swallowed by the house. The screen door reverberated like a drumbeat. Then everything settled into quiet. For several minutes chirping birds punctuated the ominous silence. Mrs. Olafson stood in her gray dress with both arms folded, patient, but both twig-like hands fidgeted as if kneading bread dough. The wide brim straw hat made her appear smaller, a worn out doll with stick-like arms and legs, but her face resembled wrinkled suede.

"We weren't doing anything except picking," 1 told her, my heart thudding in a mournful cadence. Bryna had trouble because of me. "Nothing at all."

She sounded stern. "It ain't about that, nothing t'do with ya."

After a minute, I said, "Only trying to help while visiting."

Mrs. Olafson glared. "Ain't got a thing t'do with ya."

"1 don't understand what Bryna's done so wrong."

"It's them magazines a hers," Mrs. Olafson said, close to spitting and pausing to wipe her lips with a forearm. "She's been told over again not t'have 'em in the house. She's so willful, full a spite. Like that mother a hers."

"There're only movie pictures, ma'am." My mouth went dry as I choked.

"I told Lars when we took her in," Mrs. Olafson said, now wiping her face and neck with a crumpled ivory kerchief. "His bud shouldna taken up with that woman. trash she was. Now the girl's getting the same way. Kin or not, I feared trouble."

The solemn house made me sweat even before I heard it. Not a yell, or scream. More like a fierce squeal now and then that came after a distinct snapping sound. It had to be a belt, thick leather whipping flesh. I shivered goose bumps in spite of the torpid heat. He wore a brown belt two inches wide, with a gray steel buckle. Bryna's fulsome thighs were being ravaged -- cowhide lashing girlhide.

Mr. Olafson tortured Bryna for being herself. Living in a place she didn't want to be with folks who put up with her only when she minded their ways. I squeezed a ripe peach tight in my left hand. When the agony from the house ceased, gooey pulp oozed between my fingers; the pit grated my palm. I rushed to the porch steps. Mr. Olafson came out the screen door, staring wide-eyed like someone who'd just come upon an accident. I smelled pee and saw the stained thighs of his overalls. Bryna'd wet herself, and him. I couldn't speak, but longed with childish ferocity to lash out, pitch the peach slime at him. I stumbled away down the dirt road and tried to focus through my tears on Gram's house at the edge of town, a sanctuary from hurt and guilt.

I couldn't eat supper, telling Gram what I'd witnessed. My cheeks ran wet with stinging tears. She listened as I blamed myself for Bryna's grief. If I hadn't gone, if she hadn't shown me the magazines, she wouldn't have been whipped. It was the first time I'd caused someone else pain. Gram told me not to think it that way. The Olafsons were strict Pentecosts and, like many folks, believed in severe punishment for transgressions. Most weren't as hard as Trude and Lars. I mustn't blame myself.

I stayed away from even passing the Olafson farm, going to the lake a roundabout way and eventually finding a couple boys my age to be lazy with. Three weeks later I came upon Bryna at the place where we'd first met. We chatted some, then she stripped and swam far out into the lake, surging with huge arm strokes, feet and legs kicking furious water tails behind like geysers.

I waded into the lake and soaked myself to get cool. It was early August, hot and steamy. In a month or so I'd be going back to St. Paul for school and living with Mom. Watching Bryna swim away toward the middle of the lake I recalled her telling me that these ice cold lakes were gouged out by receding glaciers and so deep in the center that they hadn't been measured. Bryna swam far out. I saw only the diminishing wake left behind before the surface closed in behind and erased her passage. A desire to lunge out there and share her anguish possessed me. But, I could never swim that distance and return safely to shore.

Soon she was on the way back, her features becoming more defined, the arms hitting the water in a rhythmic assault until her golden tresses tickled my senses every time her head swung from side to side. Much as I wanted to remain with her, I climbed out and stood drying naked behind scrub oak bushes. I watched and waited while she swam into our inlet, slowed her pace, then stood and walked to the shore, splendid in her naturalness. I loved her too much to confront her. The thigh bruises didn't seem as dark, but there were purple welts turning green. She dressed and left. I lingered like a mourner until mosquitoes drove me from the shade.

In September I returned to my divorced mother's life in St. Paul. But I spent one more summer in Arbordale. Bryna never came back from that disappearance after I'd last seen her. She'd taken a few clothes, so folks concluded that she ran off. In my mind I imagined her swimming Beck Lake's deep darkness, emerging from a sun-drenched barley field like a peasant angel, my robust girl with her painful life of labor. I wish I'd been more worthy of her and regret not being a better friend, letting her know how I felt. I sometimes fantasized that she escaped toward the gold setting sun on the rolling black prairie, all the way to movie land.

In 1955 I noted an actress in a mundane B movie —Trucker Chicks, or maybe it was Hitchhike Girls— that evoked dim twinges. I couldn't be certain, of course. But I felt undone sitting in the dark with anguished beats of my heart among strangers. Bryna, or so I hungered to believe, with a butch haircut, leather jacket, and taut jeans. Perhaps it was the exotic eyes, the brash way she dominated each scene, my farm girl assaulting gritty chores. Confident, brazen, she provoked the gang of raucous males. Everybody, actors and studs in the audience, emitted groans of lust as she strutted. Damn! Gasping for air, with clenched fists, I agonized that it was her! Wanted at last.

* * *

Ed Ford,
Lexington, MA

Arietta

There is a song in the wind
As I stand at the stern of the thrumming ferryboat
Departing from Pireas for Crete.
You are singing: Eleiason, eleiason...
You are a voice in the wind;
Curling around my ears like a whispering sea-shell
Pointing out the golden pillars of the Acropolis in the distance
High above the jumbled mass of the torrid city.
You, with your black hair and your deep black eyes,
Are a raven hovering above the white-caps
Even as the setting sun casts
Its golden wing up into the sky.
You are all the poetry of the melifluous Greek language
Mingling with the lustre of the wine-dark sea.
You are words of that great prisoner Homer
Even as you inspire my captivated devotion in 2005.
So much has happened to you and to me:
I have become far-travelled, like Odysseus,
And you have flown everywhere
On the wings of my desire
Enchanting, ennobling
Fulfilling me with the mere memory of your words
Eleiason, eleiason...
You, you are a whirling wind,
Tousling my hair, cresting the sea,
Combing the white water as the night turns it to black;
Never will I forget this moment
And how you sang to me
In the voice of a goddess
Whom only a hero could love.

Ed Ford

Love

When will I find you again?
Driving down a New Hampshire highway
I am lost amid the moiling of my memories.
The setting sun shines in columns
Through cumulus clouds that mirror snowfields
And the shadow-filled forest.
Oh, how I remember you Carolyn
And how at age eighteen
My cherished ideal was shattered
When your Camaro tried to hug a tree.
What good was all my striving
Without you to please?
I also remember you blonde Haia
Investigating French castles in the fog,
Your smile radiant
And myself too intimidated to speak.
I will never find you again,
This I know.
But at least I did find you, Arietta,
Greek queen of my heart
As the thick, winter night descended like a lid
Over the mountains of Norway,
Just days before I would set off wandering
My lonely way around the world.
Will my books ever be sold in Thessalonika
So that you might find one someday? Perhaps?
It is amazing what slim hopes we can live on.
When you are single, as I am, at age forty
You begin to wonder if anyone will ever claim you
Like a lost coat to keep them warm
On a cold night such as this.
When will I find you again?
The radio is playing softly
The song "Peaceful, Easy Feeling" by the Eagles.
I sigh and look forward to arriving home again
Where I will stay up late listening to the radio,
Awaiting the appearance in my life
Of another Venus, perpetually new,
As harbinger of dawn.

Joan Fitzgerald
Athol Springs. NY

Requiem

Hours after he watched her shadow slide under the door
he caught up with her in a bar
where she was chatting up a State Trooper.
She loved uniforms.
He was a brutish looking guy, she liked that too.
"Go home! You're tired!" she told him,
but he made his beer last three hours
until the cop gave up, the drunks wandered off
and the place closed into a powdery darkness.
The weekends were all like that now.

On this pale, dust-washed Sunday afternoon
he drove up the hill and parked off the road,
watching the hawks sweep the sky over the valley
and knew that he would kill her.
He remembered their wedding.
She, so perfect in her lace and veils
yet at the reception carrying a stuffed animal
pretending to make it talk,
they had to dance with it pressed between them,
she clutched it in the car when they left for the honeymoon
screaming out the window at the guests
"Peanut Brittle! Say goodbye! Goodbye!" waving its dopey arm
                                        and twisting its head.

And six years of high jinks with the people they ran around with,
flirting with the men,
daring one man "dance with me"
her red nails like blood flowers on his back
while their pelvises clanked
and then buying him an expensive camera
with her entire paycheck.
She loved black, black jeans,
tight dresses that exposed her breasts
highlighted her bleached skin.

There were no children.
He didn't know if he'd wanted them,
she took up so much of his time

(con't.)

Joan Fitzgerald

there was never room for much else.
The hawks were far away now,
always two —they mate for life.
The hills blurred as he started the truck
for the drive to his brother's house
where his shotgub slept in the rafters of the garage.

Printed in the United States
45893LVS00008B/16-66

9 780890 023839